Pelican Books

Polluting Britain: A Report

Jeremy Bugler was born in 1941 and graduated in
philosophy from Trinity College, Dublin: he has
worked for *New Society* and the *Sunday Times*. Since
1970 he has been a member of the Government's
Noise Advisory Council and was a member of the
working party that produced the Noise Advisory
Council's report *Neighbourhood Noise*. He is at present
Environment Correspondent of the *Observer*.

Jeremy Bugler is married with two daughters and lives
in South London.

Polluting Britain:
A Report

Jeremy Bugler

Penguin Books

Penguin Books Ltd, Harmondsworth,
Middlesex, England
Penguin Books Australia Ltd, Ringwood,
Victoria, Australia

First published 1972

Made and printed in Great Britain by
Cox & Wyman Ltd, London, Reading and Fakenham
Set in Linotype Plantin

For Sue

Contents

	Acknowledgements	ix
	Introduction	1
1	Industry's Ally	3
2	Mourn for the Mersey	32
3	The Frail Sea	59
4	Unwanted Sound	86
5	The World's Largest Brick Maker	111
6	Parks for Peace	130
	Conclusion	161
	Index	177

Acknowledgements

First, I wish to record my thanks to the *Observer* for allowing me to make use of material which came into my hands while working for the paper.

I am indebted to a number of people for help with this book, though I alone am responsible for its opinions. In particular, I wish to thank Pat Barr; Antony Buckley, Chief Water Quality Officer of the Mersey and Weaver River Authority; Gerald Leach and Laurence Marks, colleagues on the *Observer*; Kenneth Mellanby, director of the Nature Conservancy's experimental research station at Monks Wood in Huntingdonshire; Graham Searle, director of Friends of the Earth and other Friends also; Rupert Taylor; the late John Barr; Sue Masterman; David Tattersall, assistant county planning officer of Lancashire County Council; Cmdr Michael Ranken.

I am grateful, for permission to reproduce material, to Her Majesty's Stationery Office, the *Daily Telegraph*, and the Maxwell International Microforms Corporation.

I owe Audrey Brooks many thanks for peerlessly typing the chapters for no reward. Most of all, I am indebted to Sue Bugler, for both her invaluable encouragement and her willingness to take on, while the book was being written, yet more of the labours of looking after the children.

Introduction

Is pollution overtaking sex in popularity as a conversation topic? wondered a *Guardian* journalist in a week last year in which there were four major pollution conferences in London. The fearful amount of heat, talk and typing the subject generates is inescapable. Yet, curiously, it is much easier to find material that speculates on what may happen to us, rather than information on what *is* happening to us. The alternative theories about the effects of an increase in carbon dioxide in the atmosphere, speculation on whether the earth will heat up or cool down are much more accessible than information on which companies or corporations dump toxic wastes in our coastal waters. This book is intended to help fill a gap in all the lecturing and publishing on environmental damage; the absence of information on *which* company is doing the damage and *which* agency is failing to prevent it. This book aims to report more than to theorize, to describe more than to speculate.

I report therefore on the lack of effective control of industrial air pollution; on the industrial pollution of our rivers and estuaries; on the contamination of our coastal waters by industry and by municipal corporations; on industrial workers whose hearing is damaged by the noise in which they are forced to work; on land made derelict by companies; and on the new areas that industrialists have their eyes on: the last wild places of Britain. In some chapters I have selected geographical areas for particular attention, since a close report can reveal more of the nature of the problem than a broad-brush treatment. It is thus fair to say that companies criticized in the book are not necessarily the principal offenders, as far as Britain is concerned.

The book also confines itself to problems of pollution rather than resources, even though there is an increasing overlap between the two. Thus no victory will have been won if activists persuade a company to cease polluting a waterway while it continues to manufacture plastic throw-away sacking on a fuel of imported oil. Nor will an advance have been achieved if a company ceases to pollute the air while it continues to produce a cheap object with a contrived obsolescence that will demand more and more raw materials for replicas to take its place. In Britain, a coming resource crisis will demand that we change our society from a Waste State to a Thrift Society. The less raw materials a company consumes, the greater should be its reward. Fuel tariffs, for example, will have to be up-ended so that the unit cost increases with the volume of use.

But before the right prescription for a Thrift Society is found, a larger public must know the side-effects of our modern productive societies. This book sets them out, and in particular it suggests that our attempts to urge industry to clean up are sometimes aborted by a sheer 'British reasonableness'. This quality may be to some an endearing national characteristic, but the inescapable fact about the environment is that beyond a certain point, it *cannot* compromise. Dying seas and derelict landscapes show that we cannot get away with pollution. Sooner or later the ultimately intolerant environment protests.

Chapter 1
Industry's Ally

One of the first cases of direct action against industrial pollution in Britain grew out of a change of the wind. Late in January 1971 the wind blowing off Swansea Bay on to the city changed direction. As it shifted round to the east, it picked up a cargo of fine, greasy dust and dumped it a few hundred yards down wind on to some lines of poor terrace housing, plain nineteenth-century dwellings in an outer industrial suburb of Swansea known as Port Tennant. This had happened many times for many years when the wind from the east blew hard; the dust it brought blackened washing hanging on the lines, dulled the house windows and clung to the buildings. The dust was carbon black, so greasy that it needed at least detergent and hot water to remove it. It had travelled the short distance from the factory of United Carbon Black, the United Kingdom subsidiary of an American company that established the factory in Swansea after the war.

The people who lived in the terraces had protested about the pollution continuously for some years. They had taken their dirty washing in deputations to the City Guildhall; they had remonstrated with the health authorities, with the factory management and with local members of Parliament. An organization had grown out of this struggle, named the Port Tennant Anti-Pollution Association. At a meeting of the Associaton on 26 January the people decided to take the protests a stage further. A committee consisting of one person from each street was elected, the line of action was approved, and it was decided that the committee members should tell the people when to act, and at short notice, to preserve a tactical secrecy. Chairing the committee and the operation was a fifty-one-year-old steelworker Edgar Cutler. On Friday 5 February the local men and women gathered together some chairs, called for coke for a brazier and canvas sheets to protect them from the wind. They walked down towards the factory gate. Just before a narrow bridge, they stopped and set up camp across the road. Thus started the blockade of United Carbon Black, one of the first demonstrations in Britain that showed that anger at environmental pollution was not an emotion confined to the middle classes protecting their own interests.

The blockaders, and especially the housewives, stopped all trucks from entering or leaving the plant. They came briskly forward with pushchairs and children to bar the way of massive articulated lorries if anyone looked like trying to crash the barricade. The women sat around the brazier by day, shawls and heavy coats keeping out the cold; at night the men took over. The blockade was in force twenty-four hours a day. Meals were cooked on primus stoves at the barrier. Local tradesmen donated free fuel or, like one fish and chip shop, a tray of meat pies. Another shop stayed open into the small hours to feed the night-watch with sandwiches and tea.

For days and then weeks it continued. United Carbon's managers were at first reluctant to talk. They clearly believed, as the company said later, that they should not be interrupted on vital work; carbon black is an ingredient essential to the motor industry. Made by heating crude oil, it is used in the manufacture of car tyres and rubber products such as fan belts and engine mountings. But the blockade went on. The housewives especially seemed motivated by a desperate rage at having to do battle against the greasy dust that crept under their doorways, at having to hump all their washing down to the launderette because the air was too filthy to let it dry on the backyard washing lines. They had grown tired of having to argue with dry-cleaning companies about compensation when they sent unsuitable garments to the cleaner's that came back misshapen with efforts to get out the dust. Mrs Connie Jackson, the wife of a steel erector, told me at the time of the blockade 'It's disgusting. There's no other word for it. I washed my windows the other day and I was like the ace of spades when I had finished. I was *that* black, I would have been ashamed for you to see me.' Another Port Tennant wife, Mrs Margaret Dymond, wife of a crane slinger, said 'I'm not going to live in this filth no more and I don't care how long I have to stand here.'

In the event she had to stand there a good long time, but in doing so Mrs Dymond and her neighbours brought attention to a major failing in Britain's air-pollution control. They pointed out an official inefficiency that should be a matter of public debate. The blockade dragged on for days, then weeks. Some of the drivers of the lorries turned away said they sympathized. John Sharples, down from Liverpool, was reported as saying 'I think these people have got a point. It is inevitable when there is a factory like this.' The company's reluctance to talk broke down as local newspapers featured the struggle, and as the local Labour M.P., Neil McBride, made protests to the Secretary of State for Wales, Peter Thomas. On 9 February the company issued a long statement that in its formulation is a classic among the defences of industrialists hard pressed by protestors. It read:

United Carbon Black Limited are aware that the Secretary for Wales has been requested to examine pollution complaints by the residents of the Port Tennant Industrial Area and the Company would welcome such an inquiry.

In stressing they do not wish to enter deeply into the much publicized controversy, they claim their Company has been singled out for the blame and attack and feel that it will not come amiss at this time to remind the Secretary of State some facts about themselves:

1. More than twenty years ago we were invited to establish our Carbon Black business at Swansea on our present site. The Mayor of Swansea was generous in his gratitude for the well-paid employment it promised to give to local people at a time when the Government were trying to encourage industry into South Wales. This employment has since continued without break. In addition, there has been considerable benefit to local contracting companies and with people in manufacturing and installing equipment for us.

2. We were the first British company to manufacture reinforcing Carbon Blacks in the United Kingdom. Carbon Blacks are an essential ingredient in all types of car, truck, and aircraft tyres. The Motor and other industries depend on this. Without it, the car industry would quickly grind to a halt. It is used in car bodies, engine mountings, fan belts, etc. and in many domestic appliances such as boots and shoes, washing machines, plastics, printing inks, etc. Before we manufactured blacks at Swansea, it was imported at high dollar cost from the U.S.A.

3. Since we first set up in Swansea, the manufacture of Carbon

Black has turned from an art into a science. This has brought about vast alterations in Plant Design, sophisticated black collecting equipment and precise instrumentation. This especially applies to methods of preventing loss of black to atmosphere. Our company has paid particular attention to this aspect of conservation. It is more profitable to collect all we make and every practical measure available, whether in 'know how' or finished equipment has been considered. If found worthwhile, it has been incorporated in our process. Our American shareholders have the largest number of carbon black plants of any producer. They are obligated to provide us with technical advice and we make the finest use of this.

4. The Capital cost to our company of installing the most up-to-date equipment is very considerable and it is no less expensive to maintain. We know of no Carbon Black plant that has a better stack discharge performance than ours and, in this respect, we have fulfilled any promises we have made to the City Council, the Alkali Inspector or anyone else.

5. We claim our plant is operated entirely within the law and in particular fully complies with the Anti-Pollution requirements of the relevant Alkali Act under which our company is licensed.

The statement ended with observations about the number of local people who had been invited to visit the factory. It is classic because it displays without concealment, and despite the poor grammar, the thinking of a company that suddenly is asked to defend its impact upon the environment, a matter less considered when the factory was erected. It has the concern at being 'picked out'; it reminds us that it is a good local employer; it declares its work to be of national importance. But, that aside, the British sting in the statement is the company's totally truthful declaration that it had not been breaking the law and had been doing everything legally required of it, particularly by the pollution controllers, the Alkali Inspectorate. The Port Tennant people, in short, were foundering on the defence of the single most crucial pollution agency in Britain today, the inspectorate, the watch-dog of industrial air emissions.

Mr J. C. Peabody, the district alkali inspector for South Wales, with full power to decide what emissions were correct, had agreed with United Carbon Black a standard of air pollution by which he judged they were doing as well as they reasonably could. They were employing, in the correct legalism, 'the best practicable means' to reduce the air pollution. There was only one trouble with Mr Peabody's standard; it meant the cars outside the Port Tennant streets got covered in the thin film of oily dust; it meant the grass grew grey instead of green; it meant the washing problems of the Port Tennant housewives. What was right by the Alkali Inspectorate was wrong by the people in the houses in the lee of the factory.

As the blockade continued, Mr Peabody paid a visit to the beleaguered factory and inspected the equipment. His opinion was passed to the government's Secretary for Wales, Mr Peter Thomas. The opinion was that the management were adopting the best practicable means to deal with their pollution problem. Mr Thomas then said that the company was meeting its statutory obligation, as indeed it was. This news predictably angered the local people yet further. But, as the blockade neared its third week, the people waited for official action. Sensing the alarm, the inspectorate sent down from London one of its two deputy chief inspectors, Mr J. Beighton. The company prepared itself for his visit, with the plant almost completely shut down because of the effect of the blockade.

Mr Beighton came and saw, staying at the factory for three hours. His visit, though, was marred by the manner of his exit. The blockaders sat on the bonnet of his car while they asked him to let *them* take him round the works. There were 'angry scenes', reported the Welsh newspaper the *Western Mail*. But then the end of the blockade was near. The domestic strain of round-the-clock watches was telling on the people. The complexity of the solutions suggested and proffered to them was baffling.

Finally, after twenty-two days of blockade that brought the factory to a total standstill, the blockaders cleared the road. They reluctantly accepted the pledges made by United Carbon Black. The company promised to spend considerable sums on anti-pollution devices; to appoint an engineer to watch for carbon-black leakages; to set up a new housekeeping system to ensure that machinery was properly maintained. It also re-routed the lorries via another works entrance so that Port Tennant was avoided altogether. But the protestors were disappointed; they

7

had wanted the pollution stopped then and there. Their anger has smouldered on since. In May 1971 they threatened another blockade when the wind blew strongly from the east and carbon black fell again on the terraces. The management halted production until the wind changed again.

Left over from the affair is one angry remark by steelworker Edgar Cutler, one of the leaders of the blockade: 'This air pollution may be all right by the Alkali Inspector but it's no good to us.'

The affairs of the inspectorate have become more important as its power and responsibility have grown. Since 1956 when the Clean Air Act was passed, it has become prominent. The Act and the smoke-control areas it introduced broke the back of the smoke problem that produced the city smogs that made Britain infamous. (In the London smog of 1952 some 4,000 bronchial sufferers died premature deaths.) In the new critical smoke-control areas, householders had to change to fuel that made a fire without smoke; no one could burn ordinary coal. Most industrial emissions, however, were excluded from this control; they are policed by the inspectorate. This is a body that combines eccentricity, anonymity and responsibility in an extraordinary manner. It is probably the oldest pollution-control agency in the world; it was established by an Act promoted by Lord Derby in 1863. (A Royal Commission had just been held into the appalling pollution caused by sodium-carbonate (alkali) manufacturers using the Leblanc process which emitted vast quantities of hydrogen chloride into the air.) From an office in London some twenty-six inspectors cover all the industrial districts of Britain. In no telephone directory in the country can you find a reference to the inspectorate; inspectors can be contacted only if you happen to know their names, private addresses and telephone numbers. The London headquarters is a few offices in an old-fashioned, unobtrusive Whitehall office in Tothill Street. There is no nameplate on the door.

After the visitor to the inspectorate has signed a pass that the Civil Service still insist must be used, he might make his way to the office of the chief inspector, Mr Frank Ireland. A most courteous and able man in half-glasses, Ireland's progress is typical of men within the inspectorate. He went to school in an industrial area (Widnes), read chemistry at university (Liverpool) and worked for some years with a major company (Industrial Smelting Corporation) before joining the inspectorate. He is an intelligent and humorous man, and his delight in the quaint obscurity of his work is obvious. Like some of his predecessors, Frank Ireland has faced attempts to change the name of the inspectorate to something that would trip more readily off the tongue of modern man. 'Industrial Air Pollution Inspectorate' was one suggestion, to replace the literal title which actually rests in Frank Ireland himself: Chief Inspector, Alkali, Etc. Works. An attempt during the Labour Government 1966–70 to get the name changed failed. Ireland told me: 'Imperial Chemical Industries doesn't change its name just because there is no longer an empire.' The bastion fell, however, in 1971 when Peter Walker, Secretary of State for the Environment, insisted on modernity. The inspectorate fought to retain the misleading 'Alkali' in the title, and succeeded. The confusion was compounded by royal patronage and a muddling reference to clean air, though the inspectorate has no duties under the Clean Air Act. The new title: 'Her Majesty's Alkali and Clean Air Inspectorate.'

Ireland's reports, published annually, to his senior government Minister, are a curious mixture of the archaic and the highly technical. They start always with a ritual of salutations and then, in the second paragraph (always the second paragraph), a report upon the health of his inspectors.

I regret to have to report the retirement on grounds of ill-health of Mr Blank, district inspector for the area based on Liverpool. He takes with him the respect and good wishes of all his colleagues in the inspectorate and his many friends in industry and local government. With his special knowledge of pure science and his expertise on instrumentation he was able to assist many works beyond the call of his normal duties under the Alkali Act, thereby enhancing his own reputation and that of the inspectorate amongst registered works.

Then follows a list of the total of visits made by the inspectors, the numbers of committees and bodies before which the inspectorate has made an appearance, and then, always, a long investigation or lecture into one aspect of air pollution. Usually these

are most valuable or provocative, such as the details in the 1968
report of the costs of air-pollution control in certain industries in
the decade 1958–68. At other times Ireland strikes off in a
different direction. In 1969 he seemed to want to get a lot off his
chest:

Two years ago I wrote about the word 'Pollution' often evoking
strong emotional responses in all of us; indignation, strong calls for
action and clamour for the heads of officials deemed to be ineffective.
Since then the subject has become increasingly popular and has
been coupled with the name 'Environment'. Many nations have
recently awakened to the fact that the industrial revolution and the
prosperity it has brought have introduced unwelcome side-effects of
which air pollution is one of the manifestations ... But we must
beware of the obvious danger that emotions could be aroused to the
point of overriding commonsense. We have always been conscious that
this is not a problem to be tackled in a spirit of panic and those
prophets of doom who predict the more bizarre kinds of human catastrophe and paint rather self-righteous pictures of scientists as irre-
sponsible villains exploiting humanity to the point of disaster could
well be doing their (and our) cause great disservice.

After his annual treatise, whatever it may be, Ireland turns to
his review of air pollution from different industries. These are
listed under archaic nomenclature such as 'Chemical Manure' for
fertilizer, 'Muriatic Acid' works for hydrochloric acid and, until
1971, 'Paraffin Oil' works for the massive oil-refinery industry.
Often Ireland employs the valuable device of devoting special
attention to one particular industry. His reports also make clear
the disorganized way the inspectorate grew into being the industrial air-pollution controllers. The principle has been that certain
types of industries have air-emission problems too complex for
local authorities to control; therefore a national agency, the inspectorate, has been created and the complex industries are required to register with it. In Britain in 1970 there were 1,621 such
registered works, with 2,752 registered processes involved. Since
the first Alkali Act in 1863, the inspectorate has been used as a
hold-all for new industries. Revisions of the Act have given the
inspectorate control of air pollution from processes as different as
steel, the massive ammonia plants of Billingham and the huge

new power stations. At the end of 1969 there were only five operational factories which were registered for the first stage of the old Leblanc saltcake process from which the Act got its name. 'The remainder – 1,686 factories – are classed as "etc." in the title of the existing Act,' says Ireland. In this way the inspectorate has come from minor importance and obscurity to a major role – and obscurity.

If the way in which the inspectorate grew is individual, its manner of working is a reflection of the English Way so complete that it is almost pastiche. The inspectorate operates strictly within the canons of Good Form; of Gradual Reform rather than rapid change. It constantly displays a distaste for confrontation or any unpleasantness; it dislikes prosecution; it loves persuasion as much as it detests compulsion. In the pollution field it is the Keeper of Ancient Practices. It is a leading member of the Little Englanders Club. This is Frank Ireland in his 1969 report:

> In Britain there is a mixture of local and central authority control ... both are reflections of the subtleties of the English Constitution and epitomize Common Law and natural justice with their advantages over any system erected on a written constitution. They represent the continual advance by the workings of conscience and conciliation as opposed to the stagnation followed by revolution and regulation practised in some other countries ...

In this way the inspectorate shows its faith in gradualism, the drip-drip of gentle pressure. Frank Ireland told me once 'We look on our job as educating industry, persuading it, cajoling it. We achieve far more this way. The Americans take a big stick and threaten "solve your problem". We say to industry "Look lads, *we've* got a problem." In this way we've got industry well and truly tamed.'

This combination of chumminess and elbow jogging was the inspectorate's method from the first days. Ireland states in the 1967 report: 'From the outset in 1863, the first chief inspector, Dr Angus Smith, set out to gain the cooperation of the owners and to use coercion as little as possible, for he firmly believed the best results would be obtained by this method of approach.' An early letter from a factory owner to Dr Angus Smith is also quoted: 'I am exceedingly sorry I was not at the works this morning when you called. I should have congratulated you upon the success of your system of regulating chambers and towers.' The note of fear is missing.

When an industry is faced with a pollution problem, Ireland records his way of handling it. First it is offered a 'partnership' with the inspectorate in finding solutions. The firm, the inspectorate, and the industry's research associations sit down and investigate the emissions; research is carried out by the firm and the result reported to the inspectorate. 'When the inspectorate is faced with an awkward or obstructive management, the practice is to advise the trade association of the position,' says Ireland. 'Often the recalcitrant member yields to the persuasion of his fellow-members.' Failing that, there's prosecution. This Frank Ireland does not relish. Its value, he says, is public punishment and in the 1967 report he states proudly 'on only three occasions in the last forty-seven years have court proceedings been brought'. Since then, the prosecution rate of industrial air-polluters has been about two a year. These firms pay fines of about £100. In 1970 two prosecution cases were heard including one which referred to offences in 1969. They involved a tar works and a metal recovery works. Fines were £50 and £75 respectively. Most fines are paid by small companies, often backyard works burning cable to recover the metal. The industrial super-corporations, who do most of the polluting in Britain, are not prosecuted.

The method of the inspectorate, then, is 'to preserve what already exists and in particular to do nothing which might damage the goodwill and cooperation existing between industry and the Inspectorate'. How in practice does it all work out? In comparison with the worst, the British industrial air-pollution picture is not without achievements. New York averages for suspended particulate matter (smoke) in 1962–1963–1964 were 280, 285 and 222 micrograms per cubic metre. By 1968, the figure was 112·5. But the London average in 1967/1968 was 55 micrograms per cubic metre.

With sulphur dioxide, New York in 1971 was close to 0·2 parts per million. London in 1971 was 0·06 ppm. In matters of grit and dust, Ireland argues that New York still compares unfavourably with industrial cities like Sheffield: 'America is an emerging country.' But this achievement is due more to the control over domestic fires brought by the Clean Air Act than to the inspectorate.

The inspectorate has brought some better emission standards. When the electricity generating industry came under the control of the inspectorate in 1958, it operated on a standard set by the Electricity Commissioners in 1934 of 0·4 grains per cubic foot. This standard became an international standard but the coming of the inspectorate brought a fairly immediate halving to 0·2 grains. Today the new coal-fired Central Electricity Generating Board stations are pegged down to an average emission of 0·04 grains per cubic foot, though to some extent this cut is simply reflecting the much larger emissions of the new power stations, and therefore the necessity of having higher standards. With cement works, the emission standard has been reduced from 0·4 grains per cubic foot in 1950 to 0·1 grains in 1966, a reduction which would be more impressive did not the early cement works often emit clouds of white fall-out that put desert sandblows in the shade.

The inspectorate has also prompted changes in particularly highly polluting industries. The pottery works in Stoke-on-Trent once blackened the sky for miles around and made a clean shirt last half a day; when such ceramic works first came under the jurisdiction of the Alkali Inspectorate in 1958, there were 295 bottle ovens in Stoke still using smoke-producing methods of firing. A decade later none were operating, having been replaced by oil, electric or gas-fired ovens. Massive improvements have been made in the steel industry; the mustard cloud that used to pall steel towns like Port Talbot, home base of the British Steel's Steel Company of Wales division, has gone. Companies with registerable processes have tended to rationalize their plants, reducing the number of processes, or switch to cleaner fuels. Thus registerable gas and coke ovens fell from 477 to 277 in the 1958–68 decade; gas-liquor works from 140 to 81; benzene from 247 to 124; producer gas from 132 to 34; alkali works from 15 to 7; electricity works from 206 to 182; ceramic works from 585 to

384; sulphate and muriate of ammonia from 68 to 46. Clearly it would be absurd to credit all these reductions to the visits of district alkali inspectors complete with briefcases and good manners. But some credit is due.

At the same time the inspectorate has an increasing and worrying list of failures, stemming both from its over-familiarity with industrialists and from the basic principles upon which it operates. The tolerance the inspectorate can show to industry is well exemplified by the heavy-metal pollution of an area in the west of England around the Avonmouth industrial estate. The pollution came to public notice when a planning application to build forty-two houses near the little village of Hallen was surprisingly refused. Hallen is within a mile or two of the Avonmouth industrial estate, but none the less the people at the public inquiry (held in May 1971) were shaken when Dr Robert Hansen, Medical Officer of Health for mid Gloucestershire, rose and said to the inspector that his tests had shown that heavy-metal levels in and around the area where the houses were to be built were worryingly high. Hay taken from Hallen Farm showed metal levels much higher than in hay brought from outside the area. Lead levels average about sixty-five parts per million, which is thirteen times the limit laid down by the Food Hygiene Regulations. Cadmium was three to five times typical levels elsewhere and zinc averaged 212 parts per million, a high figure. Lead levels in milk taken from Hallen Farm and Kites Farm were close to the hygiene limit.

For some local people the news came only as further confirmation of a blight they had long suspected. For trouble with livestock, especially horses, is an occupational hazard for farmers and breeders in the area. Horse breeder Mrs A. Petty, who lost half her foals in 1970, has a stud farm at the neighbouring village of Compton Greenfield. 'My first two foals were affected in 1969. Then it seemed that most of them were falling down and dying, or becoming lame with horrible sicknesses . . .'

Her stable-manager, Richard Slaughter, said about his affected foals: 'After two to three months – just when they started to eat grass for the first time – their joints began to swell and eventually they could barely walk and then only stiff-leggedly.' The horses improved only when Mrs Petty moved them to thirty-five acres of grassland well away from the area. Other farmers have experienced trouble, though cattle have fallen ill rather than died.

Horses are particularly sensitive to heavy-metal poisoning and local vets are very suspicious. So is the Ministry of Agriculture. It runs a Veterinary Investigation Service, and the officer at the Langford branch, Mr Edmund Davies, has been particularly worried about the effect of the high zinc levels. It is suspected that the excess of zinc interferes with livestock's natural intake of copper, essential for health. Copper deficiency in the local livestock has been established without doubt, and copper injections are routine on many of the farms. Lack of copper can produce the kind of galloping arthritis that Mrs Petty's foals suffered. The only wild card is the fact that the local soil is peculiar for a natural excess of another chemical, molybdenum, which also is associated with copper deficiency.

Without doubt heavy-metal industrial contamination of the neighbourhood has been taking place. The possible processes in the region that might have contributed to the contamination have been under the control of the inspectorate since 1958. Matters reached a head in January 1972 when Imperial Smelting Corporation closed for improvements its lead and zinc smelter at Avonmouth, after dangerous lead levels were found in the blood of some of its workers. The government ordered a full inquiry, spurred by Bristol University scientists, who found very high heavy-metal levels on vegation near the smelters.

Another area of serious heavy-metal contamination was identified around Swansea in the sixties and published in great detail in 1971. Between 1962 and 1969 researchers from the University of Wales at Swansea carried out studies on the contamination and re-vegetation problems in large areas of waste industrial land, rich in metals from earlier operations in the nineteenth century (*Nature*, Vol. 231, No. 5301). One of the aims of the studies was to reduce the risk of dangerous heavy-metal contamination by dusts blown from smelters and waste dumps by the replanting of trees. The botany department at the university, led by Gordon Goodman and T. M. Roberts, looked at levels of cadmium, lead and nickel, copper, zinc and magnesium along sections up the valleys north and east of Swansea. They also looked at a control area including the Gower Peninsula, which is swept by the relatively uncontaminated winds coming in from the Atlantic.

The researchers took soil samples, analysed at one-centimetre intervals of depth, and samples of moss and grass, the former being a highly efficient concentrator of air pollutants, the latter less so. The results Goodman and Roberts found are very disturbing, given the fearsome effect of heavy-metal intake on human beings or animals. They found that toxic metals were concentrated in the soil ten times higher in the Swansea fall-out region than in the clean control region of Gower. Then they found that the area affected by the Swansea fall-out was larger than the area they studied – it ran out beyond thirty-two kilometres. They found that in a region near the city, the lead level in the grass was about 100 parts per million dry weight. This is above the lethal level for horses and indeed a horse died eight months after arriving in this area. A very high level of cadmium, 330 parts per million, was found in the kidney of this horse.

The study suggests, though it does not state, that the air pollution identified around Swansea was primarily due to industrial activity taking place very recently, i.e. at the time of the study. One transect ran close to a smelter in operation at the time, and a very high level of nickel contamination was found for several kilometres down-wind of the plant. No one can suggest that the Alkali Inspectorate can be blamed for heavy-metal contamination caused by Welsh industrialists buried in Methodist graveyards perhaps a century ago, but contemporary pollution is another matter. As at Avonmouth, the inspectorate had the duty to negotiate voluntary emission standards with this source or sources, as they were old works in operation when they came under the inspectorate's umbrella in 1958. Either the inspectorate has been lax in its negotiations, or it needs a power to compel old plants coming under its jurisdiction to reach new standards. If the former, the inspectorate must hang its head. If the latter, the inspectorate has defended the existing law, and has partly itself to blame.

The evidence is that the Alkali Inspectorate has been too soft with these polluters, seeing the industry's problems in close focus and the public's in a haze. Partly this stems from the beginnings of the inspectorate, in which it was often more knowledgeable about an air-pollution problem than was the industry itself. But it is also fatally due to the inspectorate's self-conceived role as an agency to help industry get on with the job, rather than an air-pollution-control agency above all. Excerpts from the reports reveal this bias: 'It is over 150 years since this country took the decision to become an industrial nation and today's major decision is not whether we should tolerate damage to amenity, materials of construction, vegetation, etc., but how much we shall tolerate it,' said Ireland in his 1969 report.

An unacademic way of finding out how industrial air-pollution is controlled is simply to drive up the M1 motorway. Near the exits for Bedford the motorist may wonder if his engine is overheating or something is burning under the bonnet. A strange and powerful smell. Probably he is sensing one of the by-products of the brick-making companies in the massive Bedfordshire brickfields. Forests of chimney stacks – about seventy-five of which are active – emit volumes of sulphur dioxide and also amounts of fluorine and gases (probably mercaptans) that cause a 'rubbery' odour. All these gases are potentially harmful or unpleasant.

Without question Bedfordshire brickfield country is one of the most polluted parts of *rural* England. The release of sulphur dioxide has been shown by the county medical officer to give this area of trees, fields and chimney stacks the atmosphere of a small industrial town. The county medical officer, Dr M. C. McLeod, avers that he would never advise a person with bronchial difficulties to live in this part, even though the exact effects on human health are hard to quantify. (A comparison between residents from the brickfield area and residents outside was not conclusive, as the cigarette-smoking habits of each group were not included.) Trees appear to languish around the brickfields; there is an abnormal amount of stag-headed, stunted growths, taking on sometimes what the late John Barr in *Derelict Britain* (Penguin Books, 1969) described as 'thalidomide shapes'. Contemporary evidence suggests that these results may be partly put down to the corrosive sulphur dioxide. Bedfordshire's county planner, Geoffrey Cowley, has examined the state of the vegetation in the brickfield with great care, noting and mapping the dead or dying species. 'There is visible decay to stand testimony to the decline in the quality of the landscape,' he wrote in his report *Bedfordshire Brickfield* (1967). In the same report he says: 'Evidence from this country, however, does suggest that where the degree of wind exposure is high the effects of industrial air-pollution, including the sulphur and fluorine compounds, are intensified. These result in the browning of foliage leading to subsequent loss of vigour and ultimate dieback of the tree completely, giving a stag-headed appearance.' The dying of the trees cannot be put down to air pollution solely or with complete certainty. Cowley mentions other possible causes, such as changes in the water table. The level appears to have been lowered perhaps by the brick companies' clay-working activities, and also by a changeover from stockfarming to arable farming. (Such a changeover can also harm trees and hedgerows through deeper ploughing.) Cowley does however record that certain air-pollution *resistant* species – elms, willows and poplars – have done well in the brickfield country.

The brickfield chimneys are more clearly at fault through their emission of fluorine compounds, which can cause appalling damage to livestock. The compounds fall on the grass; cattle which eat heavily contaminated fodder go down with fluorosis, a kind of bovine version of rheumatoid arthritis, but involving additional bone damage and dental decay. Many brickfield farmers have suffered from fluorosis-damaged herds. For three years in the 1950s the Ministry of Agriculture, Fisheries and Food launched a major investigation into fluorosis in cattle. The reports appeared in two parts, published in 1964 and 1965.[1] Investigators from the Central Veterinary Laboratory found that in the Bedfordshire area nineteen out of forty-three farms investigated were affected by fluorosis severe enough to lose the

1. Part 1: Fluorosis in Cattle – Animal Disease Survey Report No. 2, H.M.S.O., Part 2: describes how economic farming can be done in a brickfield.

farmers money. Of the nineteen fluorosis farms, three had abandoned grazing in favour of arable farming, eight were severely affected and eight were slightly affected. This whole situation is summed up in a quiet phrase from the 1965 Alkali Report: 'There is a farming hazard.'

Farmers have reacted to the threat in two ways. Some have changed their agricultural practice, switching to crops and taking their herds to market. Others have made double sure that their cattle have a substantial amount of brought-in food, and they do not repeatedly graze the same meadow. The London Brick Company itself has a highly successful herd at Stewartby Farm, very near brickworks. It points to the Smithfield honours its herd has won, and says that by good husbandry any local farmer can emulate them. Many of the local farms, in fact, do belong to London Brick and are leased to tenants.

But despite the terrible damage of fluorosis, the Alkali Inspectorate has worried most about the rubbery brickfield smell. Perhaps shrewdly it has considered that people would still complain about the air pollution if the fluorine were tackled but the smell remained.[2] No doubt people would, and they would be quite sensible to do so. Smell is a real pollution, as county planner Geoffrey Cowley is reminded when he is faced with planning decisions in the brickfield areas. 'The smell is such that I couldn't place an old people's home there or a hospital. The smell restricts our planning freedom,' he says. Local people who have lived in the brickfield for years no longer notice the smell, probably for the good physiological reason that their ability to sense certain odours atrophies after continued exposure. But, for those with noses to smell, the brickfield odour is both pungent and unpleasant.

What has the Alkali Inspectorate done to curb these three pollutants – the sulphur, the fluorine and the malodour? Its principal method has been to get the brick companies to build their chimneys higher, the idea being to spread the gases more widely. Where new brick kilns are being built, the chimney stacks now top 300 feet. But many of the older brick kilns cannot take

2. 102nd Annual Report on Alkali, etc. Works by the Chief Inspector, 1965. All Alkali Inspector reports are published by H.M.S.O.

the weight of taller stacks and it is clear that the brick companies want many more years' service out of their old faithful kilns. So a very high level of dispersion is not being attained. London Brick monitors the ground-level concentrations under the instructions of the Alkali Inspectorate. The chief inspector concludes that levels of sulphur dioxide and indeed the fluorine concentrations 'continue to be satisfactorily low'.

Sulphur dioxide, however, can be removed as well as dispersed. The Wood River power station in Illinois uses a Monsanto Cat-Ox process to 'wash' the fumes, and it recovers marketable sulphuric acid, as well as pleasing its neighbours. The Cat-Ox process, however, would not suit the brickfields. Such is the immense quantity of gases emitted that it has been calculated that it would need the entire ten-million-ton capacity of Stewartby Lake near the London Brick headquarters to wash less than a week's emissions. A water-pollution problem would anyway be created to replace the atmospheric one. As a general principle, I would declare that a company should operate only if its pollution load is insignificant, irrespective of its economic importance or factors such as contribution to exports. But it is argued the Bedfordshire brickfield should be an exception. A local peculiarity in the clay from which the bricks are made allows the bricks to be markedly cheaper than clay products from other fields. As a contribution to the housing needs of Britain, the Bedfordshire bricks are a great resource.

Flettons hold up the roofs of countless houses in Britain; this bed of clay running from Huntingdonshire into Bedfordshire provides about half the bricks made in Britain. The Bedfordshire flettons, most of them produced by the London Brick Company, account for about a quarter of Britain's bricks.

Any 'pollution dispensation' cannot exist for long. Experiments in manufacturing bricks from waste products, including ashes, glass and any old iron, are most hopeful. Types of 'waste bricks' are being marketed. If they could undercut the flettons, the brick companies would clearly lose their pollution privilege. Waste bricks, after all, would be a re-cycling of material, a better use of resources than stripping the soil from the fields of Bedfordshire.

No real excuse exists for the Alkali Inspectorate in its handling of the brick companies' emissions of fluorine compounds and the special nasty 'reek'. The smell is an elusive chemical, thought to be mercaptans, though no one is certain. But it has been established that the smell is created during a stage preliminary to proper baking, a combustion stage when the bricks are heated to between 100°C and 700°C. During this 'coming-hot' stage, the troublesome pollutants come off the clay. Obviously enough, it has occurred to some people that pollution problems could be solved more easily if the combustion 'coming-hot' gases could be separated from the drying gases and treated. As it is, they mix in with the drying gases in the massive kiln chimney and the concentrations of smell, sulphur dioxide and fluorine are made far too dilute to be removed.

London Brick researchers have found on an experimental basis that the combustion gases *can* be separated from the drying gases. But they have not discovered how they can be treated. In 1971 they were examining a process referred to them by the Alkali Inspectorate, which has been applied on a small pilot basis in the United States. The process is designed for sulphur dioxide removal not for the smell constituents or fluorine. A magnesium oxide 'cake' is used as an absorber of the sulphur dioxide; the theory is that if the plant is close to a sulphuric acid works, the 'used' cake, now magnesium sulphide, would be taken to the acid works and there regenerated into magnesium oxide, whereby the cake would be returned to the polluting plant. London Brick's staff did not start looking at this idea until October 1971, and it is obvious that the investigation is at the very earliest stage. Chief research officer Dickie Richards told me 'We're only at a pilot stage – about the same as when we had a look at the Cat-Ox process before.'

The evidence is strong that the Alkali Inspectorate has not pushed London Brick into finding urgently a solution to pollution problems. Dickie Richards told environment journalist Jon Tinker in 1971: 'The problem is to find a method of treatment. If someone had a process which showed some promise, we'd be prepared to have a go at it. We look into any new ideas that turn up. It isn't that there are things to be done and we are refusing to spend the money.' Jon Tinker castigated the company for this attitude and asked if it was satisfactory for a company with a £25 million turnover to wait for ideas to turn up.[3] My own discussions with Dickie Richards were no more comforting. He told me: 'The company has not done any work removing fluorine apart from a scheme to put lime in the process to remove it. That didn't work. The company's main work has been to see the effects of the fluorine *after* it's left the chimney.' He added: 'Up to the moment, no practical economic method of removing sulphur or fluorine has been found.'

But my case is that the company has not done enough work to remove the fluorine, or the sulphur dioxide or the smell; experimental work has not proceeded beyond the first stage. It has had treatment processes referred to it, and it has examined these without trying very hard to develop its own treatment processes. London Brick may be excused for not solving the sulphur-removal problem single-handed – it is a massive problem and the company has some of the most unsuitable chimneys in the country. But one might have expected the company to allocate considerable sums to continuous week-in, week-out research to cut down the problem that has caused a great deal of concern to local farmers, and the problem that mars the amenity of the brickfield country. But some responsibility for this failure rests with the Alkali Inspectorate.

From a first reading of its references to the fletton industry in the inspectorate's 1971 annual report, Ireland's staff might be thought to be making real progress. It says, 'In 1971 it is expected to commission a new kiln fitted with steam flues which can be connected to an outside extraction system, whereby the best practicable means for dealing with hot gases can be investigated.' In fact, says Dickie Richards, there is no immediate plan to investigate the best means of treating the hot gases bearing the pollutants; the new flues have been fitted in case, in future, such a method of treatment should 'turn up'. But the inadequacy of the inspectorate's armoury is made clearer by examining that phrase 'best practicable means'. This is Ireland's crucial legal phrase. If ever the inspectorate went republican and jettisoned the Royal

3. *Daily Telegraph Magazine*, 28 May 1971.

Coat of Arms, its new crest would bear the inscription 'Best Practicable Means'. On the Day of Judgement, it is believed alkali inspectors present themselves before the Almighty and aver they have employed the Best Practicable Means.

Under its enabling legislation in the various Alkali Acts, the inspectorate is empowered to force companies to use 'the best practicable means' to prevent the emission of noxious or offensive gases and to render harmless any of those gases that have necessarily to be discharged. That is the theory of it all. The phrase is nowhere in the Alkali Acts precisely defined, but it is defined in the Public Health Act 1936 and the Clean Air Act 1956 in this way: 'practicable' is taken to mean reasonably practicable having regard to local conditions and circumstances, to the current state of technical knowledge, to the financial implications and to compatibility with any duty imposed by law. 'Means' is taken to be including the design, installation, maintenance and manner and periods of operation of plant and machinery, and the design, construction and maintenance of buildings.

The long and the short of these phrases is to take interpretation of what is 'best practicable means' out of the hands of the law makers and into those of the inspectorate and, in the very rare cases of prosecution, into those of the local magistrates. Fatally, the words tend to get interpreted as meaning 'the cheapest practicable means', and they do not place any obligation for the polluting company to *find* the best practicable means. If the means for removing the gas is well known, you can rely on it the Alkali Inspectorate will see that it is installed and used by scheduled factories. But if the means for efficient prevention has not yet been discovered, the effect of the 'best practicable means' phrase is to allow primacy of industry's desire to produce (and pollute) over the need of the environment to remain uncontaminated.

An astute defence, the best in the circumstances, of the phrase has been provided by chief inspector Frank Ireland:

> If economics were of no consequence, there would be very few, if any, problems of air pollution control which could not be solved readily. We have the knowledge and the apparatus for absorbing gases, arresting grit, dust and fumes and preventing smoke formation. The only reason we still permit the escape of pollutants is because

economics play such an important part in the word 'practicable' in the expression 'best practicable means' and most of our problems are cheque book rather than technical.[4]

In a give-away sentence, Ireland recounts that the finest arrestment plant seen by the inspectorate is at a works recovering rare metals such as platinum, palladium, osmium along with commoner metals such as gold and silver. Says Ireland 'The efficiency of arrestment was close to 100 per cent.' One is not surprised.

The phrase, in short, reflects the economic convenience of industry. It is by no means adequate to prevent factories from passing on or externalizing their air-pollution costs to the local population in terms of soured amenity or higher laundry bills or lowered health. The phrase is of the age the Alkali Inspectorate was born in – the great era of Victorian industrial expansion, achieved at appalling social cost to the bulk of the working populations of the time and to much of the landscape of Britain.

Only four classes of industrial works have 'best practicable means' spelt out to them by law: statutory standards (generous in nature) are laid down for alkali works, factories emitting hydrogen chloride, and two classes of sulphuric acid works. The inspectorate itself seems to have been aware of the wide range of interpretation that 'best practiable means' is open to for all the other numerous works under its control. To help industrialists it lays down also 'presumptive standards' that have no real legal validity but tell industrialists that if they meet with these standards, the inspectorate will presume that their factories are employing the best practicable means to abate air-pollution. The setting of these presumptive limits indicates the personal power of the chief alkali inspector. One of Frank Ireland's former deputy inspectors, E. A. J. Mahler, wrote in an appendix to the 1966 report that the setting of these limits is 'entirely at the discretion' of Frank Ireland. But Mahler hastened to add, 'This does not mean they are necessarily set in an arbitrary fashion.'

Nor indeed are they. The limits are arrived at after bargaining

4. Address to the Second International Air Pollution Conference, Washington, D.C., December 1970.

and talks between the inspectorate and the trade associations, and a review of the technology controls. There is much merit in these types of limits. Statutory standards can be altered only by the laborious process of getting Parliament to revise the legislation; but presumptive standards have the advantage that they can be altered at will by the chief inspector to 'take account of improving technology and the demands of the public for a better environment', to quote Frank Ireland himself, speaking at the Second Air-Pollution Conference held in Washington, D.C., in December 1970. The presumptive standards are also set in a manner which copes much better than the statutory limits with the twin aims of the act – to limit *both* the emission of noxious gases *and* to make sure that the gases necessarily discharged are harmless and inoffensive.

There are just two difficulties with this process of presumption and agreement. First, the limits would be much more valuable if they were less sweeping; if 'best practicable means' could be re-drafted so that in certain circumstances an industry could be required to *find* a solution to its air-pollution problem – in its own laboratories, with its own funds – rather than rest its case on the current state of technology in air-pollution control. A schedules list should be drawn up of particularly dangerous pollutant, and any factory with an emission greater than a stated quantity could be required to hunt out its own solution. The presumptive limits would then be used mainly to police industrial emission of pollutants not scheduled in this manner, and also to revise the limits of the new scheduled pollutants. These changes would make sure that large corporations could not evade pollution control merely by spreading their hands and sighing that no one had come up with answers yet.

The other drawback of presumptive standards is connected to their advantages: they depend upon the ideals, motivation and behaviour of the people enforcing them. Because of the obsolete thinking *vis-à-vis* industry of the inspectorate, the interpretation of standards at the moment is not working to our advantage. In his paper E. A. J. Mahler succinctly sums up the 'philosophy underlying the present choice of standards': 'No emission discharged in such amount or manner as to constitute demonstrable health hazard in either the short or long term can be tolerated.' That sounds fine, but read what follows:

Emissions, in terms of both concentration and mass rate of emission, must be reduced to the lowest practicable amount. The determination of what is practicable demands striking a balance between technical possibilities on the one hand and costs on the other. The technically possible would be impracticable if the costs were so high that the manufacturing operation were thereby rendered unprofitable or nearly so.

But would London Brick have been rendered unprofitable if it had been required to find a solution to its fluorine problem? In the case of the United Carbon Black factory in Swansea, the inspectorate's interpretation of what was practicable afforded some comfort to the American shareholders of that company, but it gave little to the working-class terrace dwellers who live beneath that factory's plume. Besides, though the company says it had ordered new pollution-control equipment before the blockade, the demo did speed improvements. The company, since then, has not been rendered unprofitable. One can use this evidence to confound the inspectorate without drawing upon the much larger argument: should a company be allowed to pollute in a major manner, even if a full air-pollution control *would* put it within the chilly embrace of the Official Receiver? The tenet that industrialists really should behave in a manner that does not permanently damage the environment is what conservation is all about.

But the Alkali Inspectorate conceives its roles as 'in partnership' with industry. It knows that 'there are no generally agreed formulae for calculating chimney heights, nor any sound, scientifically based standards of waste gas concentrations which must not be exceeded at ground level' (Frank Ireland). It knows therefore its role in adjudging standards is vital. But since it is a self-conceived partner, not an independent judge, its standards are not objective. It is caught between serving industry and serving the public, and at present it is industry that has been getting the better of the deal. Frank Ireland has set out how an inspector in the field may work in his Washington speech: 'Inspectors are made as autonomous as possible and each man goes into a works as the personal representative of his chief inspector with full authority to negotiate and reach agreement. Occasionally inspectors are faced with difficult propositions by managements and may wish to study the problem or even consult headquarters, but, in the main, inspectors are able to reach decisions across a desk or on a site, or with but a minimum of delay. 'It is this ability', Frank Ireland told his American audience, 'to take responsibility and give quick decisions which pleases industry in its negotiations with the inspectorate.'

Even when it does show awareness that industry's pollution practices are in general deficient, the inspectorate still shows a preference for bromide solutions. The 1971 report argues that all industrial plants that are big enough should have their own specialist teams devoting their time to the factories' environmental problems. 'These should be headed by a senior member of staff who can insist on the various operational sections carrying out their environmental protection duties correctly.' Sound, but hardly at the very heart of the problem. Frank Ireland's other principal piece of advice to industrialists in the 1971 report is to improve their public relations. 'We have always encouraged works to be as frank as possible about their emissions with local authority officers, the Press and the public, within the limitations of commercial confidence,' he said. 'The inspectorate is not free to release information without the permission of the owners.' Free flow of information, like more research, is a cause no one can oppose. But Ireland should really have produced more guides to new industrial air-emission policy than calls for new company appointments and better public relations.

There are further specific cases to show that affability and personal power can cut the wrong way. Rio Tinto-Zinc, the multi-headed international mining corporation, applied for permission to build an aluminium smelter on Anglesey, near the town of Holyhead, in October 1967. The proposal was hotly contested at a public inquiry because aluminium smelting causes emissions of fluorine, the same chemical that causes problems in the Bedfordshire brickfield. R.T.Z. told the public inquiry of the standards of emission of fluorines and gases. The emissions were quite moderate, and it is reported that the figures 'had the effect, desired or not, of making the County Council and the public begin to wonder what all the fuss was about. A letter from the Alkali Inspectorate was read, expressing deep satisfaction with the way in which R.T.Z. were preparing to deal with the problem of controlling these effluents, and eventually the entire matter was left in the hands of the inspectorate' (Richard Thompson Coon, the *Ecologist*, June 1971).

R.T.Z. got their planning permission, constructed their huge aluminium smelter, now run by Anglesey Aluminium Company, a subsidiary in which R.T.Z. have a majority shareholding. Very late in 1970 the smelter went into production; but a few months before this the information leaked out that the Alkali Inspectorate had allowed R.T.Z. to treble the gaseous emission of fluorides from the main stack over the limit the company declared at the inquiry. Total emissions were found to be exceeding the inquiry levels by 54·7 per cent. These are major changes, particularly worrying in view of the extremely dangerous effects of fluorine, called by Dr Kenneth Mellanby, director of the Nature Conservancy's research station at Monks Wood, 'the most serious of all the air-pollutants'.

The Alkali Inspectorate's one justification for this alteration is that the height of the chimney stacks at the smelter was increased. Originally there were to have been two stacks – the main one of 300 feet and one for the anode plant of 125 feet. Now all the emissions (except some from potroom louvres) leave through a single stack, 400 feet in height. Frank Ireland would argue that the increased height and the increased dispersion that it has given is just as good as the previous arrangements. This is unconvincing. Climatic conditions – perhaps a severe inversion – can readily concentrate pollutants, and the more the pollutants, the greater the concentration.

The whole incident distressingly reveals the inspectorate's final priorities. Ireland wrote in November 1970 an astonishing letter to a local resident, Mrs M. I. Biggs, who complained at the change in standards. The letter is worth taking sentence by sentence:

'We do not accept that the estimates submitted by the

Company at the Public Inquiry were binding in any way.' (A point R.T.Z. and the inspectorate tactfully did not stress at the inquiry.) 'They were given in all good faith as typical of what emissions were expected in order to meet our targets, on which the figures were based.' (Nonsensical circularity.) 'They represented our preliminary estimate of what might be achieved on the evidence of known technology.' (Objectors at the inquiry do not remember this tentativeness expressed then.) 'The important point of the Inquiry, in relation to air-pollution, was that the company should meet the requirements of the Alkali Inspectorate.' (The inspectorate, however, had no compulsory powers over aluminium smelters at this time.) 'When we got down to details of design and in the light of practical tests carried out in the U.S.A. on full-scale plants, it soon became obvious that we had to change our original thoughts on prevention and dispersion in order to keep the project viable.' (An acceptance that aluminium production took precedence over the environment protection. The public inquiry was the instrument for deciding whether the project should go forward, not the private agreements of the inspectorate.)

The letter continued:

'The important point, which you seem to miss, is that it is the effect of the emissions at ground level which matters most and not the mass emission of pollutants.' ('Dispersion can never be an alternative to prevention,' said Ireland to his American audience at the Second International Air-Pollution Conference in Washington, D.C., just over a month later.) 'In this, our requirements have not changed and the environment is safeguarded just as much under the new conditions as under the old, perhaps even with a minor improvement.

'Industry cannot be handicapped by rigid rules based on estimates.' (Of what value then is an assurance to a public inquiry?) 'There is hardly a major product which is not altered between the original plan and completion, even when construction is proceeding. The Alkali Inspectorate's system is geared to take care of such changes and I see no reason why the Anglesey Aluminium Company should be penalized in a way which applies to no other works.' (The government cannot have agreed with its chief inspector, for eight months later it placed all aluminium smelters under the *statutory* control of the inspectorate.)

Frank Ireland's closing remarks did not comfort Mrs Biggs:

'I feel sure that there will be further changes in plan as the site develops and the professional expertise of the inspectorate will be fully used to give acceptable conditions to the community. We have looked as far ahead as we and the company can visualize. Like any practical situation, there may be times when operations are upset by abnormal circumstances and *no guarantee of immunity can be given.* [My italics.] On the technical side we shall see that all practicable precautions are taken to keep such incidents to a minimum.'

It is perhaps in statements not made to a public audience that people most reveal themselves. Personally, reading this letter convinced me as much as the angry, distressed faces of the Swansea housewives that the role of the inspectorate needs radical revision. The inspectorate must abandon its meek conception of itself as 'a partner'. It must conceive itself as an industrial air-pollution police force: its role being to protect the public, to see that laws are enforced and miscreants duly punished. To inspectors such a change will not come easily. In a nutshell Frank Ireland and his inspectors must become more answerable to the public. As a beginning, the workings of the inspectorate should be open to the public gaze. District inspectors should have district offices, with names and addresses in the telephone books, and employees to answer, person to person, inquiries from the public. The local district inspectors should also make regular reports to the county councils, municipal and borough authorities in the area over which they have jurisdiction on the standards they have required of local manufacturers. This same information should be open to any member of the public who requests it.

The name of the inspectorate should be changed (again) to something less opaque to the man in the street: Industrial Air Pollution Agency is a possibility. This agency should have its own separate head office in London, employing press and public-relations officers rather than using the general facility of the Department of the Environment. The style of the reports should be changed radically, abandoning the archaic device of the letter to the Secretary of State, throwing out redundant nomenclature, so that fertilizer is called fertilizer and not chemical manure. The reports should include passages in simple clear language to explain the import of all the major sections; the necessary technical details can be imparted separately, in a smaller type, within the same report.

One absurdity that must go is the 'ten years' grace' given to a company or industry newly scheduled to be controlled by the inspectorate. For the first ten years of 'partnership', the company is only under 'voluntary' obligation to comply with the inspectorate. And then there is the ludicrous number of inspectors – 26 – to control the industrial air pollution of one of the most developed nations in the world. Many more inspectors must be recruited.

If these changes of style were accompanied by the changes in the legislation I have mentioned in this chapter, we might forge an adequate air-pollution agency. The era of 'understandings' reached behind factory gates is over: laws should not only be enacted but seen to be enacted. And in fact there is a solution to the inspectorate problem that could well be resorted to, if the changes I have suggested are deemed insufficiently radical. This is to return the power to police industrial air emissions to the local authorities and their publicly elected representatives. The inspectorate could continue to exist as an advisory organization, to be called in by the local authorities when the public health inspector needed specialist advice on a technical problem. Such a solution makes the blood run cold alike of industrialists and the inspectorate. The former dread the break-up of a special relationship; the latter understandably cherish their independence. The public, for whom the state of air is becoming of as much importance as the rate of production, would welcome the change-over. It should be borne in mind by future legislators.

Chapter 2

Mourn for the Mersey

New Brighton is a seaside resort in the North-West, built right in the British tradition, with a promenade, funfair, boarding-houses and a pier. It has also some more unusual attractions. A curious mock castle, now given over to dodgems and discothèques. And on the tide excreta, balls of fat, sewer scum, rotting vegetable waste, contraceptives. In summer children have been seen bathing amid flotillas of these objects. On winter days people strolling on the promenade itself have had to watch their feet to keep their shoes clear of crude sewage. But then New Brighton is on the Mersey Estuary.[1]

At near-by Rockferry old sewage and marine rubbish is stranded on the high-tide line. Fat and oil especially gets trapped in a corner near the promenade. Fresh sewage is always floating on the tide. But then Rockferry is on the Mersey Estuary.[2]

At Magazine Village, if you want to walk on the beach, you may have to cross a solid band of organic matter, mainly fat, and a yard wide, stranded on the high-tide line. Again sewage floats on the tide. But then Magazine Village too is on the Mersey Estuary.[3]

The Mersey is the paradigm of a standard British practice; using estuaries as super-troughs. Every day forty-five factories, refineries and industrial plants release fifty-two million gallons of trade effluent into the estuary, much of it in a poorer condition than would be permitted for a river discharge.[4] It is also a massive unflushed lavatory. Every day seventy-three million gallons of raw, crude sewage are discharged from ninety-five separate outfalls.

The estuary as a whole and New Brighton beach in particular are the end result of a massive river-basin pollution. What floats on the tide, what greys the water, what destroys the life-essential

1. Report on the Condition of the River Mersey Estuary and the Adjacent Coast Line, Mersey and Weaver River Authority, 1971.
2. ibid.   3. ibid.   4. ibid.

oxygen in the estuary is an accumulation of small paper and textile mills fouling headwater streams in north-west Lancashire, of antique sewage works in the lowlands, of oil refineries on the fringe of the great cities, and then at the last the estuary factories and sewage pipes. The catchment areas of the Mersey and Weaver Rivers contain some of the worst fresh-water pollution in the United Kingdom. Study of them indicates the kind of task we face when we talk about restoring the polluted areas of Britain.

As well as direct discharges of effluent the Mersey Estuary accepts the flow of the River Mersey, the rancid Sankey Brook, the River Gowy draining the refineries of Ellesmere Port and the badly polluted discharge of the River Weaver. These rivers are the principal drains of the massive north-west conurbation. The River Mersey arrives daily with a cargo of 205·1 million gallons of sewage effluent and 105·2 million gallons of trade waste. The Weaver chips in with a daily contribution of 15·2 million gallons of sewage and 84·4 of trade effluent; the Gowy adds 0·3 million gallons a day of sewage and 3·0 million gallons of trade effluent.[5]

Treatment on this scale inevitably has its effect. Huge volumes of waste make heavy demands upon the estuary's oxygen. The River Mersey alone flows into the estuary with a pollution load measured in terms of Biochemical Oxygen Demand (B.O.D.) of 117,000 lb. a day.[6]

That figure indicates the absolute minimum amount of oxygen the river needs to destroy waste by natural processes, and return to a full, oxygenated, healthy state. If the dissolved-oxygen level falls, the river's self-purification processes are hampered; fish cannot survive, and waste, instead of being destroyed by natural aerolic processes, starts to putrefy. The water stinks if the level falls close to zero. Every summer samples taken by the Mersey and Weaver Authority's pollution officers at a sampling point on the estuary known as 'I.C.I. Widnes' show that dissolved oxygen has fallen to zero.[7] This is true of most of the stretch of water between Warrington and Widnes.

5. ibid.   6. ibid.
7. Mersey Estuary Report, Table B.

What has happened to the Mersey Estuary can be said also of almost every major estuary in Britain, with the exception of the Solway. The Tees Estuary receives about 500 untreated discharges and is a horror; yet before the First World War it was a good salmon river.[8] The estuary of the Tyne collects every day ten million gallons of industrial effluent and thirty-seven million of raw sewage, from 270 outfall pipes in all.[9] Not only does the Tyne Estuary suffer grievous bacterial pollution, but a survey by researchers from Newcastle University has shown that pollution extends five miles out to sea.[10] As for the Severn, forty per cent of Welshmen in Wales (1·1 million people) have been flushing their sewage into it, plus their industrial waste. 'Only seven of the discharges are fully treated and nine are partially treated, out of a total of ninety discharges.'[11]

The Usk, Ribble, Wear, Humber and Thames Estuaries are all badly polluted. The Thames is contaminated by partially treated sewage from local-authority works, presenting more than 500 million gallons a day of sewage effluent. The full national picture may best be presented by the painstaking River Pollution Survey of England and Wales 1970, by the Department of the Environment and published in December 1971. This showed that 862 miles (48·1 per cent) of estuary were clean, 419 miles (23·4 per cent) were doubtful, 301 miles (16·8 per cent) were poor and 209 miles (11·7 per cent) were grossly polluted. This state represents no improvement at all on figures from an earlier, more informal survey undertaken by the Ministry of Housing and Local Government in 1958. The amount of poor or grossly polluted mileage was slightly higher in 1970 than in 1958, though one should not press comparisons too hard since the surveys were not identical. However, the mileage (28 per cent) of poor or grossly polluted estuary is shown by the 1970 survey to be very much higher than that of the rivers (9 per cent).

Much of this grievous damage can be put down to one factor: an expansive loophole in pollution-control powers of river authorities. Currently they are about as powerful as a pensioners'

8. *Taken for Granted*, Report of the Working Party on Sewage Disposal, chaired by Mrs Lena Jager, 1970.

9. ibid.   10. ibid.   11. ibid.

club when it comes to their ability to force a restoration programme upon polluters. Under the Clean Rivers (Estuaries and Tidal Waters) Act, 1960, the river authorities have control only over new discharges or those that have been radically altered since 1960. The long-standing polluter is protected; if he was fouling the estuary before 1960, he cannot be prevented from doing so today. These existing effluents are by far the major portion of estuary pollution, especially in the Mersey Estuary. Strategies for cleaning up just cannot be implemented.

The results are visible on the estuary beaches like New Brighton and Magazine Village. So gross is estuarial pollution that it was selected by the Royal Commission on Environmental Pollution in 1971 as a subject for its first in-detail study. During 1971 members of the commission visited a number of estuaries to prepare a report, expected to be published in 1972. Commission members will have observed physical demonstrations of the lesson that pollution costs money, that it not only causes what river-authority men term 'nuisance', but that it also damages a resource. Putting it another way, the local authorities and the companies that discharge poorly treated waste into our estuaries are doing so at someone else's expense.

The Tyne demonstrates this graphically. While a quarter of a million people live within a mile of the banks of the final sixteen miles of the Tyne Estuary, the estuary itself is a recreational disaster. Excreta cling to the foreshore; the water stinks. The bathing beaches near the mouth of the estuary are fouled – you can see the pollution at times. Very high coliform counts have been found between the piers at North and South Shields and in both instances the muck coming down the estuary is to blame.[12] Most of the tidal Tyne is poor or grossly polluted, according to the River Pollution Survey of England and Wales, 1970 (H.M.S.O., Vol. I, p. 13).

Recreational troubles also affect the Thames; as *Taken for Granted* says, the problem may be highlighted by the Greater London Council's new town on the estuary banks, Thamesmead. The town dwellers have been told that 'the river will be at their

12. ibid., p. 25.

doorstep – part of their way of life'. They may grow to regret it.[13]

Shellfisheries suffer severely from estuarial pollution. Oysters, cockles, and mussels and clams and scallops live by filter-feeding, which concentrates particles in their bodies. In polluted water they concentrate sewage bacteria, which is why some shellfish are so dangerous to human consumption. And why the Public Health (Shellfish) Regulations were passed in 1934, allowing local authorities to ban the sale of shellfish from polluted grounds.

This power has been used to ban oyster fishing in the Lynher and Tamar Rivers. Other oyster fisheries have had pollution problems, including Whitstable and Poole Harbour, the Rivers Roach and Colne and Upper Blackwater.[14] Mussel fisheries have been disturbed, very badly in the Wash, but also at Morecambe, Exmouth and Lytham. *Taken for Granted* estimates the costs, noting that 'actual and potential value of shellfisheries has been severely reduced by pollution'. In France 1,400 million oysters were sold in 1967 at a value of £23 million, while the United Kingdom water produced only five million oysters a year, say the Shellfish Association of Great Britain. Polluted estuaries also prevent salmon and trout fishing in the whole length of the river, as the migratory fish balk at entering the fouled water.

Mersey Estuary pollution takes its toll in the damage to the beaches described at the start of the chapter and in other, less obvious manners. But in order fully to understand how this estuary is so damaged, it is necessary to begin at the beginning, to start at the headwaters of the rivers that drain into the estuary. The estuary itself is only the end-product of a severely polluted river basin.

The rivers of Manchester and Widnes and Liverpool transport the sewage from over five million people, the population of the north-west conurbation. And they convey the effluent both of small manufacturing firms and some of the largest industrial complexes in Europe. Shell Chemicals at Carrington issues waste into the River Mersey; the effluent pipes from Manchester's

13. *Tomorrow's London*, Greater London Council, 1969.
14. *Taken for Granted*, p. 26.

Trafford Park Industrial Estate, with its flour millers and detergent makers and oil refineries, run into the Manchester Ship Canal, which at that point is the River Irwell canalized. The rivers to the north and west of Manchester carry the trade waste of papermills and textile plants, of bleachers and piggeries, dyers and tar works, wool manufacturers and chemical companies.

The Augean stables, perhaps, were lightly fouled compared to the Mersey and Weaver Authority's province. Almost a third of all the sewage effluent is unsatisfactory or bad. Of the 156 factories putting what is called 'trade effluent' into the rivers (not the estuary) more than half were unsatisfactory or bad and only thirty-two had satisfactory discharges, says the authority's annual report for 1970–71.[15]

The river authority, one of the more progressive in Britain, annually provides a guide to the health of its rivers, a map at the back of its annual reports. Bravely the authority classifies rivers into four groups; clean, poor or doubtful, bad, very bad. The clean sections of the rivers are marked blue on the map, like in any schoolboy atlas. Poor rivers are marked yellow, bad are red and very bad are black. Look at the map, and unlike in the schoolboy atlas, these rivers are rarely blue. With the exception of a few brooks, the blue rivers are short stretches of headwater, changing colour as they meet their first industry. It's a thin blue line indeed. Exactly 65 per cent of the Mersey and Weaver Authority's rivers need treatment; 35·1 per cent or 340 miles of them are poor or grossly polluted.

The four gradings are tightly defined. A 'clean' river is drinkable after normal treatment, supports fish, and *looks* clean. It has a biochemical oxygen demand (B.O.D.) not normally exceeding three milligrams per litre. (The B.O.D. test was given the stamp of officialdom by a Royal Commission on sewage disposal in 1912. It refers to the amount of oxygen consumed by the breakdown of matter in the water over five days at 20°C. Anything over ten B.O.D. is very much to be sniffed at.)

A 'poor or doubtful' river no longer looks clean, needs more treatment before it can be drunk, rarely supports fish and may contain traces of toxic chemicals. The B.O.D. does not regularly

15. Mersey and Weaver River Authority Annual Report, 1970–71, p. 40.

exceed eight milligrams per litre. A 'bad' river is quite unsuitable for drinking, cannot support fish, has the nasty qualities of a 'poor' river plus the attribute, in summer, of having some reaches of the river almost totally devoid of oxygen. A 'very bad' river is a real hydro-horror. It is visibly grossly polluted, and in summer the sluggish reaches are devoid of oxygen. The average B.O.D. is normally greater than twelve milligrams per litre. (These definitions vary slightly from the standards used in the River Pollution Survey of England and Wales, 1970.)

Trace part of the basin's network of rivers, and the industrial role in 1971 becomes clear. The most northerly streams are the headwaters of the Irwell. One stream, named the River Ogden, after a short distance collects the effluent of the Holden Vale Manufacturing Company, makers of cotton linter.[16] The company has installed equipment to settle and control the acidity of effluent; but in 1971 Holden Vale were discharging an effluent containing bleach waste into the stream. The classification of the stream declined downstream of the works. The other principal headwater meets industry first in the form of the Loveclough Printing Company – part of English Calico Limited – near the town of Rawtenstall.[17]

Classification of the river declines downstream of the works. As the headwater streams build up into a single river, the classification is only 'poor or doubtful'. This is no mean standard for the Irwell and is the acme of its achievement from source to mouth, leaving aside those little pristine, fledgling headwaters. Once at this stage the river was classed 'bad'. Some of the improvement was due to action from a sewage board, whose name is an exercise in northern syllabics: the Haslingden, Bacup and Rawtenstall Outfall Sewage Board. The board in 1970 completed major extensions and modifications to its sewage works at Ewoodbridge, putting it back about £1 million. Now the works properly treats about five million gallons a day of sewage and trade effluent that once damaged the river.[18]

The Irwell ambles on into the town of Ramsbottom. It meets

16. Mersey and Weaver River Authority Annual Report, 1968–69, p. 98.
17. Mersey and Weaver River Authority Annual Report, 1969–70, p. 86.
18. ibid., p. 87.

the effluent of the Ramsbottom Bleaching and Dyeing Company, a dyeing and finishing waste. Shortly after, the river accepts the effluent of the Holcombe Paper Mill.[19] No river rejoices at meeting a paper mill; they use vast quantities of water (perhaps 50,000 gallons to make a ton of paper) and the effluent usually contains paper fibre. This fibre sinks to the river bottom and decomposes, using up oxygen.

After taking sewage from the Ramsbottom Sewage Works and effluent from the dye works of T. Robinson and Company (dyers and finishers) – who started work in 1969 on a new treatment plant[20] – the Irwell flows south, with a classification of 'poor or doubtful'. At the town of Bury it picks up sewage effluent, waste from Olive's Paper Mills[21] and bleach waste from A. C. Bealey's bleach works at Radcliffe.[22]

The river deteriorated markedly in 1971 after a meeting of the waters with the River Roch, which throughout its course was 'very bad', that is, visibly grossly polluted. The Roch conveys 18·7 million gallons a day of trade or sewage effluent, from overloaded sewage works and from bleachers and dyers, papermills and other works.[23]

The Roch's effect on the Irwell is to generalize the classification 'very bad' to both rivers. Flowing on, the Irwell takes seven million gallons a day of sewage effluent from Bury Corporation (of a good standard) and then papermill effluents from the East Lancashire Paper Mill[24] and the Radcliffe Mill.[25] Both effluents consume some oxygen from the river.

Shortly after, the Irwell meets its second major tributary, the River Croal. It comes bearing a cargo of crude sewage from overloaded sewers, and paper and bleach effluent. In its short course, the Croal remained in 1971 for most of its length with a 'very bad' standard, rising to 'bad'. This 'improvement' is in fact a deterioration – in 1969 the Croal was only poor or doubtful on its last lap. A deal of the pollution is due to 'storm sewage' – when

19. 1968–69 Report, p. 98.   20. 1970–71 Report, p. 80.
21. loc. cit.   22. op. cit., p. 97.
23. 1968–69, 1969–70 and 1970–71 Reports.
24. 1970–71 Report, p. 79.
25. loc. cit.

heavy rainfall causes sewage to overflow into emergency storm pipes, then into the river.

The Irwell now enters an increasingly industrial landscape: ranks of power-station cooling towers, wrapped in steam, march across the line of sight; the acreage of waste and derelict land, the grass a sallow yellow as if the natural green were too ambitious, is massive. Some of us, being fortunate in the beds we were born in, do not have to live in this shattered landscape that gives us wealth. If we did, we might wonder more about the price.

Now winding through the outskirts of Manchester, working itself towards the heart of the city, the river receives waste from an Electric Power Storage factory,[26] where Exide batteries are made. Treatment plants have reduced lead pollution in the waste to a low level. Next offering is sewage effluent from Prestwich sewage works, seasoned with chemical waste from Magnesium Electron[27] on the opposite bank, warmed up by the cooling water discharged from the Agecroft Power Station and finally discoloured by mine water pumped up from the pits of the National Coal Board's Agecroft Colliery.

The slight heating of the river by the Central Electricity Board's power stations, at Agecroft and again at Kearsley, is not particularly damaging to the Irwell, for it is so despoiled anyway that heating is a minor assault. In some rivers, however, power stations do cause real damage to river life, particularly in some long, slow-moving continental rivers where power stations line the banks like anglers. Since each returns vast quantities of water – up to fourteen million gallons an hour – heated 10°C by being used to cool generators, the whole temperature of the river is gradually warmed up. River life becomes threatened when this heating combines with hot summer and low summer flows; after a certain temperature rivers lose oxygen much more quickly.

But for the Irwell, it's a pinprick. Much more serious is yet another fetid tributary, the Irk, whose flow is sometimes entirely composed of sewage and trade effluent. The 1971 condition of the river was 'very bad' from within a mile of its source. And the River Medlock, joining the Irwell stream a mile downstream, is

26. 1968–69 Report, p. 98.
27. 1970–71 Report, p. 80.

little better – polluted especially by the waste from piggeries and raw sewage flowing out of storm sewage pipes.

Manchester is ashamed of the Irwell. You can tell that by the way the city tucks the river away in the back streets, encloses it between high warehouse walls, and never runs an open street beside it. But the city none the less needs the Irwell. Quite near the city centre it takes its water from the Pomona Docks. Then under a swing bridge and the Irwell finds itself enclosed between man-made banks and renamed the Manchester Ship Canal. In fact, it's still the Irwell and it has a few miles of life in it yet. It skirts the Trafford Park Industrial Estate, collecting cooling water from companies like Procter & Gamble, and Brown & Polson, and spillage from Esso and Burmah, and at Davyhulme picks up the immense flow – sixty-eight million gallons a day – from the sewage works, culmination of countless Mancunian flushings.

Canalization has slowed the river flow and now it is very nearly completely deoxygenated. But trudging westward, through the industrial horror of Salford and Eccles and the blasted western outskirts of Manchester, it comes to Irlam, and becomes a tributary itself, giving up its identity to the River Mersey.

It's a helluva way to run a river. Almost from source it has failed to fulfil what some would regard as part of the definition of a river: a stream of water capable of sustaining life. At the end of its progress, it has accepted 146·2 million gallons a day of sewage effluent from thirty sewage works and 35·4 million gallons a day from the fifty-six factories that line the Irwell and its tributaries. The final Irwell flow is more than seventy-five per cent effluent. The modal or usual flow is 223 million gallons a day, 181·6 of which are effluent. What is it? A river or a conduit channel?

Yet it is not by any means either the most polluted or the only severely polluted river system in the area. The Sankey Brook that flows through St Helens is a shocker, with a maximum recorded Biochemical Oxygen Demand in 1970–71 for 165 milligrams per litre – an astonishing figure. It sometimes is thick with suspended waste. (A clean river does not exceed three

B.O.D.) British Sidac of St Helens, makers of transparent paper, contribute to the pollution and in 1970 were considering installing a new effluent-treatment plant.[28]

The River Alt, to take another example, was worse in 1971 than ten years before. Its first major effluent problem is from Liverpool Corporation's North Sewage works, about four miles from its source at Huyton. The effluent from the works is roughly twenty times greater than the flow of clean water available in dry weather to dilute it. From this point on, any natural self-purification in the river is wiped out by more effluent discharges – including the waste from Peerless Refining Company, a large fat-processing factory.[29] Storm sewage completes a mucky picture.

And what is the effect of the massive use of Lancashire rivers as trade drains and toilets? Well, obviously enough, it completely negates any possibility of the rivers being pleasant natural features which in a pleasurable way could be used by the local people. The fishable rivers of the Mersey and Weaver Authority can be counted on the fingers of one hand. As for bathing in the rivers, a policeman was once disturbed enough to see me standing by the banks of the Irwell to get out of his car (in the rain) and plead 'Don't fall in there. You'll ruin my afternoon.' No family in its right collective head would picnic on the banks of a river like the Roch. For a community this inability to be able to use its natural watercourse in natural ways is a grave recreational loss. You may also wonder about the loss to the senses in being required to live in an area where the landscape is violated.

There are other, measurable losses. The area is, remarkably for a place where the rain falls close to the national average, running short of water. In 1967 1,468 megalitres a day were drawn from the statutory water authorities. By 2001 2,737 are expected to be drawn – almost double. To meet this deficit, the master planner of the nation's water-resource development, the Water Resources Board, is examining numbers of schemes. They include the very real possibility of estuarial storage at Morecambe Bay, Solway and the River Dee and large inland reservoirs. Certainly one or

28. 1969–70 Annual Report, p. 84.
29. 1970–71 Annual Report, p. 75.

other of these two types of storage, and possibly both, will be required. Both types are expensive, and bring special problems of their own.

The trouble is that the rivers, the numerous rivers, that flow through the North-West are too polluted to be used for anything else than industrial purposes – and sometimes too polluted for that too. And the region's aquifers, the natural underground reservoirs where water is held between strata, are also badly abused by industry.

The principal aquifer concerned is the Permo-Triassic sandstones. The amount of groundwater that is naturally fed into this aquifer has been assessed at between 100 and 127 millimetres over the recharge area. According to the river authority's painstakingly careful 'First Periodical Survey' of water supplies,[30] these quantities are much less than the amount now sucked up by industry and by the statutory water authorities. Liverpool is abstracting forty-one per cent more groundwater than the feed to the aquifer; the Wirral is overdoing it by forty-three per cent; Warrington exceeds its mark by thirty per cent, Gowy by twenty-nine per cent. All these places would have to cut back their abstraction by these percentages to balance with the supply.

The effect of this thirst? Well, something has had to give, and the answer is the aquifer itself. Because so much water has been drawn up, the levels of underground water have fallen below sea level. Now highly saline water has moved into the aquifer. This has been going on for a long time now and not surprisingly the river authority is worried stiff about it. It is after all a savage comment on industrial rapacity to find that a borehole sunk some distance inland brings up sea water.

The aquifer scandal is part of the same scheme of things as the river pollution: the needs of industry being given total ascendence over the needs of the community. Indeed, the north-western malaise is the common and desperate fallacy that the interests of industry and community are one and the same.

This has meant that the rivers of Lancashire are by and large not suitable for drinking water. More than that, it has meant that valleys in the Lake District – like Haweswater and Thirlmere –

30. Mersey and Weaver River Authority, 1969.

and in North Wales have had to be flooded or adapted so that Liverpudlians and Mancunians can drink. Some of the Lake District schemes have been national scandals and carried out only because the thirst of Manchester is deemed to be stronger than the objections of the Friends of the Lake District. Welsh schemes like Llyn Celyn have again roused ferocious displeasure. Welsh nationalists understandably object to the flooding of valleys in their country to keep the taps flowing in another. For so long have places like Manchester lived off the soft water from the hills, brought by aqueduct, that it would be difficult to convert to using hard-water supplies drawn from the river. But it would not be impossible to override this taste; indeed, Mancunians might be encouraged to look more kindly upon hard water when they realized that hard water absorbs less of dangerous metals, like lead. The main obstacle to using the region's rivers for drinking water is in fact once again industry.

The fact is that the effluents of modern industry are becoming increasingly complicated and harder to analyse. The effluents, more and more, contain chemicals in very small quantities but yet very dangerous. The Institute of Water Engineers in 1970 reported increasing concern over the presence of such chemicals in water supplies. Work by two Liverpool University researchers, J. A. Tolley and C. D. Read, has added to this disquiet. Sometimes some of the more socially valuable industrial processes produce very difficult effluents: the flameproofing of children's garments, for example.

Of course this is no reason why such polluted effluent should go into the river, but in terms of practical politics, firms have been putting their effluent there and will go on doing so. And at the same time, these effluents will probably contain more and more chemical traces that are very hard, if not impossible, to remove in the normal water-treatment works and also very hard to discover if they are present. For this reason, very few north-west rivers will be able to be used for potable purposes. This is realistic, though all very sad for the Lake District and North Wales.

What Antony Buckley, the Mersey and Weaver's Chief Water Quality Officer, *can* do is to restore his rivers to a state where fish can live in them and the streams are no longer a sensuous insult to the local people. His strategy is twofold. The first attack is upon overloaded, outdated sewage works. His rivers carry vast quantities of sewage effluent, and much of it is of a poor quality. In other words, it has not been treated to the level at which it will not cause deterioration in the river. Sometimes the sewage is settled only – the solid waste alone removed. Getting local authorities to spend money on sewage works is a hard furrow to plough. Some still believe that there are no votes in sewage, and in areas where gross pollution of the environment has been the order of the day for generations maybe they are right. But by cautious and persistent prodding the Mersey and Weaver Authority has made some advances. Its scheme has been partly to encourage centralization in sewage works, so that the smaller units with inadequate staff are eliminated. During 1970–71 four small works were closed down in the authority's area and connected to large schemes. On top of that, twenty-seven sewage works in 1969–70 had improvement schemes carried out. Thus the Irwell benefited from an improvement to Ewood Bridge Works, the unit in the early part of its course, under the Haslingden, Bacup and Rawtenstall Sewage Outfall Board. Then the demise of the appalling Mount Sion Works at Radcliffe was a factor in the restoration of the Irwell. As for the future, the Roch will cheer up when the Roch Mills sewage works at Rochdale are reconstructed.

But it is more than just a matter of sewage works. Sewerage schemes often have to be rebuilt, and progress here is also tied to the amount of money coming forward from the local authority and the loans from the central government. Rivers in the North-West often get polluted by 'storm sewage' or by antiquated sewers that leak. Where possible, the authority has been trying to get separate sewage and surface-water sewers built. The trouble with the standard combined drains-and-sewers system is that heavy rain either hampers sewage treatment, or it causes untreated sewage to overflow direct into streams and rivers. For a reasonable system in their areas large parts of Manchester and Salford will have to be re-sewered.

On the success of the first attack upon dilapidated sewerage rests also the success of Buckley's second attack. This is directed against factory effluent, the stuff that for years the businessman thought he had a right to add to the local river. The weapons Buckley has to hand exist principally because of a private member's bill which successfully ran the parliamentary gauntlet and passed into law in 1961 to become the Rivers (Prevention of Pollution) Act 1961. Together with a 1951 Act, sharing the same bureaucratic title, this legislation requires any firm or concern that wants to put its effluent in the river to seek a 'consent' from the river authority. The river authority then has the power to fix conditions to the consent – to say it will allow the discharge only if the B.O.D. is of X standard and the suspended solids of Y standard. These conditions can be appealed against to the Department of the Environment. In the past, when the department did not exist, and the Minister of Housing was the final arbiter, firms often found it worthwhile to appeal. Since pollution has become a live issue, the ministerial court is less favourable.

The consent device does give the river authority a mild grip around the offender's throat, the technique being to set time limits on the consents; a polluting firm is given a few years at the end of which it will be expected to reach a certain standard in its effluent. The screw can then be tightened further. This method has been manifestly successful: for example, most textile and paper mills that line the banks of the Irwell have been steadily improving their effluents.

Where he does not get improvement in the factory's own treatment system, Buckley tries to get the firm to send its effluent for treatment to the local sewage works. He prefers this tactic because he does not have total confidence in the way some companies run their treatment plants; often they do not have specially trained staff for the plant – it is just another responsibility of the overburdened works manager. At sewage works, however, Buckley can be reasonably confident that the effluent will be well treated, given a good sewage works in the first place and a competent management staff backed up by the local authority.

More and more firms in Buckley's area now do send their effluent along to the local works. Qualitex Yarns of Radcliffe used to be an Irwell polluter; now the effluent goes to sewer, the firm having paid for the interconnecting pipe.[31] Shell Chemicals sends the more polluting waste from its massive Carrington plant to treatment at Manchester Corporation's Davyhulme Sewage Works, paying between 15p and 20p per 1,000 gallons treated. The River Irk now has a much greater chance of behaving like a river now that polluting effluent from J. Chadwick & Sons of Chadderton goes to the local-authority sewer.[32] The River Irwell will be improved also when Radcliffe Paper Mill's effluent eventually goes to sewer.[33] And so on.

However, there are snags in sending trade effluents to sewers. The major one is caused by those effluents that contain chemicals that knock out the bugs in sewage works that do the noble work of decomposing the material (the 'activated-sludge process', by name, and invented in the last century at Manchester's Davyhulme Works). But by and large the link between factory and sewer is a fruitful one. The proof can be found, of all places, in the Irwell itself. The river is not a pleasant one, but it has been improving its complexion slowly, especially since the passing of the 1961 Act. Once even the upper reaches before Rawtenstall were polluted by textile effluent; now they are clear. And, though throughout most of the remainder of its length the Irwell is 'bad' or 'very bad', it is not as nasty as it was. This is proved by looking at B.O.D. values along its length. In 1961 at Ramsbottom the average B.O.D. value was fifty (remember a clear river has a B.O.D. value of under four). In 1970 the reading at Ramsbottom was six. Where the Roch joins the Irwell, a 1961 reading showed the B.O.D. to be 82, against a 1971 value of 16·3. At the Croal confluence downstream a 1961 average B.O.D. was a vertigo reading of 134; in 1971 the value was 7·7.

A great swell of optimism should not overtake you as you read these figures. For one thing B.O.D. is not a foolproof guide to the cleanliness of a river. The River Weaver gives the lie here. On the B.O.D. standards of the august Royal Commission on Sewage Disposal of 1912, the lower reaches of the Weaver would be assessed as fairly clean. But in fact the water contains a great deal of dissolved solids and ammonia, plus a high pH value

31. 1968–69 Report, p. 99.   32. 1969–70 Report, p. 90.
33. 1970–71 Report, p. 79.

(acidity–alkalinity reading) so that the water is not even fit for agriculture or industry, apart from cooling purposes. For another thing, some of the North-West's rivers like the Alt have actually got worse, thanks to the Liverpool Corporation's North Sewage Works and the fact that, though some effluents have got cleaner, *more* effluent in total is going into a river with a relatively low flow. The Alt is the alternative to the Irwell.

Yet, by and large, the Mersey and Weaver River men are cleaning up their rivers. Taken altogether, the campaign is working. It won't, of course, be complete enough to avoid more expensive and perhaps undesirable reservoir schemes being undertaken to feed the taps of Manchester and Liverpool. But it will, in the long term, give back to the North-West rivers with fish and life within them. Now that's no mean feat.

The task will be simplified by a courageous decision taken by Peter Walker, Secretary of State for the Environment, to reorganize water services. He announced in December 1971 that he intended to jettison the existing multiplicity of bodies and agencies that control water supply, sewage, water conservation and the waterways. In place of these 1,400-odd bodies he decided that ten regional water authorities should be created. They will deal with water services 'literally from the source to the tap', based on the natural river basins. Such boldness was unexpected – the decision flew in the face of many local authorities, jealous or proud of their own control over their own water supplies and sewage.

The change, which will come into effect on 1 April 1974, will greatly strengthen the pollution controller's hand. In future a company discharging effluent to a sewage works will always be charged a direct rate for the job. While some companies today already pay such charges, for many their effluent treatment is merely borne by the rates. The new charges should help into reality the slogan 'make the polluter pay for the pollution he causes'. The authority that provides the industrialist with effluent treatment will also provide him with clean water. The authority will thus be concerned that its waterways are not polluted, since the natural waterways are by far the best way of transporting water. Today it is not always in the interest of a local authority to re-build an inadequate sewage works – after all, the polluted water flows downstream and into a neighbouring borough. After April 1974 all the sewage works in a natural basin will be administered by the appropriate regional water authority. In short, the whole water cycle is properly to be administered.

But when the River Mersey tumbles over Howley Weir in Warrington, setting up a great froth of detergent foam, the reparative strategy of the river authority collapses, on account of the tenderness shown to long-term polluters by the Clean Rivers (Estuaries and Tidal Waters) Act 1960. Antony Buckley of the river authority is left with the task of trying to get local authorities and industrial companies to spend large sums of money by dint of moral persuasion alone. The hottest gospeller would be unequal to this task.

Estuary water, down from Howley Weir to Helsly Hale, is in the 'very bad' classification. From there down to an imaginary line between Birkenhead and Liverpool, the water at low tide is classified as 'bad'. Only as the curious narrow neck of the estuary starts to open out into Liverpool Bay does the classification improve to 'poor'. And these classifications hold despite the twice daily flushing by million upon million gallons of sea water.

Only one solitary mile of the river authority's estuary mileage is clean. Three miles are doubtful, forty miles are poor and twenty-three miles are grossly polluted. In all, ninety-four per cent of the Mersey and Weaver's non-tidal waters are badly polluted – and nearly all this mileage is in the Mersey Estuary.

Aldermen, city and borough councillors are much to blame. The map on page 50 gives the amount and state of the sewage the Merseyside towns contribute to their own riverfront. Some local authorities – such as Warrington, Widnes, Runcorn urban and rural district councils, Whiston, Ellesmere Port borough council and Hoylake borough council, have treatment or improvements to their sewage disposal in hand.[34] Others are conspicuous for their idleness. Bebington borough council had no plans to reduce the pollution load of its sewage – about 9,000 lb. B.O.D. a day – other than storing it to discharge on the ebb tide.[35] Crude

34. Mersey Estuary Report, Table D.
35. ibid.

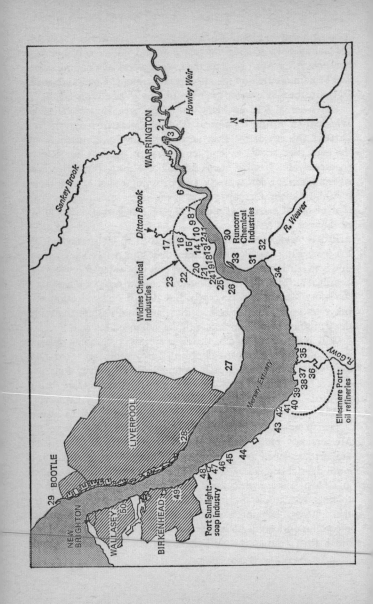

1   Thames Board Mills, Warrington. Huge effluent including paper fibre. 6 million gallons a day (m.g.d.).
2   British Aluminium, Warrington. Effluent with suspended solids. 0.325 m.g.d.
3   Laporte Industries, Warrington. Effluent contains chemicals, in particular hydrogen peroxide.
4   J. Crossfield & Sons (Unilever). Large soap effluent, part with high B.O.D. 2 m.g.d.
5   Warrington Sewage Works. Settled only. 5.5 m.g.d.
6   C.E.G.B. Fiddler's Ferry Power Station. At full capacity: 36 m.g.d. Cooling water heated 7°C.
7   Bush Boake Allen. Chemicals in effluent.
8   Widnes East Sewer. Untreated. 3.1 m.g.d.
9   Croda International. Chemicals in effluent.
10 United Sulphuric Acid Company. Large volume of effluent.
11 Fisons Industrial Chemicals, Widnes.
12 I.C.I. Pilkington Sullivan Works. Large quantity of effluent from manufacture of Grannox Weedkiller with significant amounts of suspended solids.
13 Fisons Fertilizers, Widnes.
14 Thorium Rare Earth, Widnes.
15 I.C.I. Gaskell Deacon Works and Mond Research Laboratories.
16 Barium Chemicals, Widnes.
17 Laporte Chemicals, Widnes.
18 Mersey Casings & By-Products Ltd. Animal-fat effluent.
19 Grannox. Animal-fat effluent.
20 Albright & Wilson, West Banks Works. Large volume of effluent containing chemicals.
21 Forrestal Industries, Widnes. Tannin effluent.
22 Ward Blenkinsop & Company, Widnes. Chemicals in effluent.
23 Golden Wonder Crisps. Potato-starch effluent with oxygen demand.

24 William Olroyd/Croda International. Animal-fat and glue effluent.
25 Widnes West Sewer.
26 Whiston R.D.C. sewage outfalls. 1.4 m.g.d.
27 McKechnies.
28 Liverpool Sewage Outfalls. 35.2 m.g.d. Untreated highly polluting sewage and industrial effluent.
29 Bootle Sewage Outfalls. 5.5 m.g.d. Untreated sewage.
30 } ⎫ Wigg Works.
31 } I.C.I. ⎨ Castner/Kellner Works. ⎬ polluting effluent.
32 } ⎩ Rock Savage Works. ⎭
33 Runcorn Sewage Outfall. 1.4 m.g.d. untreated sewage.
34 Frodsham Sewage Outfall.
35 Shell (U.K.) Stanlow & Shell Chemicals. Large quantity of highly polluting effluent.
36 Burmah Oil. Polluting effluent including oil.
37 I.C.I. Dyestuffs.
38 Associated Octel.
39 Vauxhalls. High-standard effluent.
40 Bowater's Mersey Mill. Large volume of effluent, including paper fibre.
41 Kelvinator Ltd.
42 Van Den Berghs. Oxygen-demanding effluent with fats.
43 Associated Chemicals Company.
44 Lubrizol.
45 Bebington Sewage Works. 3 m.g.d. of untreated sewage.
46 Food Industries Ltd. Food waste in effluent.
47 Prices, Bromborough.
48 Unilever, Port Sunlight. Large volume of effluent with soap and detergents.
49 Birkenhead Sewage Works. 7 m.g.d. of untreated sewage.
50 Wallasey outfalls. 3 m.g.d. of untreated sewage.

sewage and sludge that the city fathers of Liverpool permit to be discharged into the estuary is the biggest pollution load of all the estuary bears – a massive 146,000 lb. B.O.D. a day. In 1971 there were no plans to treat this effluent, and it would be many years before any sewage plants in Liverpool could be built, even if the city had started planning in that year.[36] Bootle, Crosby, Birkenhead and Wallasey also had no plans in 1971 for treatment.[37] Yet if the Mersey Estuary is to be substantially cleaner at the end of this decade, considers Antony Buckley, all these councils will have to build full- or partial-treatment works by 1978 at the very latest. Expenditure will be very heavy, and engineering problems complex. Councils will have to pay and commission several miles of intercepting sewers to pick up the scores of outfalls and discharges. Major upheavals to roads and private land and buildings will have to be borne. As an indication of the price, an intercepting-sewer scheme has been prepared for Tyneside, with an estimate tag of £30 million upon it. But money must be spent; councils that at present do not have treatment works in hand are precisely those responsible for the faeces in the New Brighton water, the contraceptives floating amidst the sandcastles on the beaches.

The labours of Buckley will be no less hard when he turns his attention to the estuary's industry, which contributes a daily pollution load of 206,000 lb. B.O.D., part of the total direct pollution load the estuary receives of 475,000 lb. B.O.D. We have seen that Buckley has little power. He can come down on new or substantially altered discharges. Theoretically speaking, he can also apply to the Department of the Environment for an order to control a new discharge. But such application for orders has not been an effective control method – only fourteen such tidal-water orders have been made, few in major estuaries, since the orders were introduced by the first river pollution act, the 1951 Rivers (Prevention of Pollution) Act. The reason is the laborious nature of the method and past unhappy experience with Whitehall arbitration. Often a lengthy and costly public inquiry is necessary for such an order.

The light of publicity can be a sharper weapon than appeals to

36. ibid., p. 5.   37. ibid., p. 5.

an industrialist's conscience. Lobbyists for British industry, however, did their best to try to minimize the amount of information available to the public. Pressure in the drafting stage of the 1961 Rivers (Prevention of Pollution) Act bore fruit in Section 12 of the Act. Under it, any information about the content or quality of a factory's waste which passes between the firm and the river authority cannot be given to public or press. Justification for this legal gagging is the argument that details of one company's effluent could inform a rival of trade secrets, manufacturing processes and so on. There's little truth in this one – it is a popular myth that the acutest industrial spies should look not in boardrooms but down drains. What is wrong is that commercial considerations get precedence over the public's right to know and over the counter-argument that environmental health cannot be assured unless facts are available.

I decided to counter this information block by writing directly to all the companies who discharge waste into the Mersey Estuary. I wanted to know of each company the character of its effluent, treatment processes, plans for future treatment, and how much had been spent on effluent control. Some never replied. Others were very helpful and invited me for visits to their factories. Yet others replied in the full tradition of Section 12, the secrecy clause. Two factories side by side on a dock estate at Widnes belong to the Smithfield and Swanenberg group. Both manufacture edible fats like sausage casings.

Replying to me, J. Chambers, managing director of Mersey Casing & By-Products Company Limited, wrote:

Whilst we have every sympathy with your study and appreciate your wish to obtain as much detailed information as possible, we feel that against the background of continuous improvement and change it would be confusing to be specific about our methods and plans for dealing with effluent at any given point in time.

Sister company Granox Limited, just over the road, were little more forthcoming. After felicitations, managing director R. Bee wrote:

The publication of the precise details for which you are asking

53

would, we feel, enable our competitors to catch up with us at a fraction of the capital outlay which we have incurred. All the information you are seeking is available to the relevant authorities operating under current legislation and we are assured that our past and future disclosures of confidential information will not be disclosed to any outside body.

Fisons Industrial Chemicals, also in Widnes, agreed with Grannox. Unit manager J. P. Birkinshaw wrote that he was unable

to give you anything which is helpful since to go beyond merely stating our consent conditions with the Mersey River Authority could well indicate the routes we use in our manufacturing processes. . . . I am sure you understand that being in a highly competitive industry we have to take a very strong line as to what we make known outside the Company.

Fisons say their plans, long and short, include treatment so that their effluent is 'acceptable' to the Mersey.

Price's Chemicals of Bebington found that

although, in principle, we are not averse to rendering such assistance as we can to studies of the kind you are proposing to undertake, it is necessary for us to keep our staff to an absolute minimum and it would, therefore, not be possible for us at this present time to provide you with the detailed information that you have requested.

McKechnie Chemicals, who manufacture and refine copper products at Widnes, took me very literally. 'We do not discharge effluent into the Mersey Estuary,' wrote managing director R. G. White. In fact, the McKechnie effluent runs into a stream which after a short distance reaches the estuary. Pressed further, McKechnie could only 'regret we cannot see our way clear to providing the information you are asking for'.

But many companies who replied did send information, not all of it as chemically complete as one would have wished. None the less the setting and solution of the Mersey problem becomes more clear. The surge of public interest in environmental pollution has caught many firms unaware and now they are faced with severe problems. Some are like Ward Blenkinsop, chemical manufacturers, appropriately sited in Widnes, cradle of the British chemical industry. When the Ward Blenkinsop factory was built in 1939, it was 'at a time and in an area where the evils of effluent were scarcely considered', to quote general manager T. I. J. Toley. The factory layout meant that effluent was discharged with little treatment apart from removal of superficial oil and the addition of lime into a stream known as the Ditton Brook. Then the brook combined the roles of open sewer and industrial drain, carrying coal washings from upstream, and chemical effluents along its course.

When mines closed, the Ditton improved slightly, and Ward Blenkinsop found itself with an inappropriate factory now expected to come clean. The company has major problems because of dairying effluent. Sensing a new public feeling breathing down its neck, it has begun to make changes. Some effluent will go for treatment to the local sewage works; the remainder will be treated in a company plant (under construction in 1971) for removal of all oils and tar, suspended solids, and neutralization, so that the effluent is neither strongly acidic nor alkaline. The bill, says the company, will be about £71,000.

In other industries effluent treatment can be more costly. Bowater's Mersey Mill is a case study of the problems of manufacturing in the environment age. Effluent from the mill's newsprint machines and ground-wood mill is collected in a common sump which discharges into an open basin beside the Manchester Ship Canal, and then syphons under the canal to flow into the estuary. Anything up to fifty tons of china clay and 150 tons of woodpulp fibre is discharged by the mill each week (1971 performance).

But Bowaters are reluctant to clean up beyond the point where it is self-financing, i.e. would pay for itself in recoverable materials. The company told me:

Treatment as a pure exercise in environmental improvement, however, can scarcely be viewed as anything but wholly unproductive and prohibitively expensive.

Nevertheless, as responsible citizens Bowater executives, amongst whom there are amateur yachtsmen, biologists, wild-life enthusiasts and the like, recognize the vital social implications of the problem.

But there's a limit to this responsibility, for the company goes on:

As working members of an already hard-pressed industry, however, they are understandably reluctant to countenance the almost wholly unproductive expenditure of huge capital sums without some form of tax relief, investment grant or some other financial incentives to their company, or indeed to British industry as a whole.

A depression falls on the mind as one reads such statements. They indicate a general inadequacy among profit-maximizing, privately controlled industry to harmonize with the environment except where there is a profit to be made. Bowaters demand public subsidy to prevent themselves from polluting the public environment.

Significantly, the Mersey Mill is a pre-1960 plant and there-fore beyond the river authority's statutory control. Age is a good indicator of the worst estuarial polluters. Ellesmere Port, with its serried ranks of refineries, contributes a massive pollution load of 103,000 lb. B.O.D. a day. Principal contributors are Shell U.K.'s Stanlow refinery and Burmah Oil plant. Last year they made up the bulk of the Ellesmere Port area's discharge of 10·2 million gallons a day of trade effluent. Both refineries pre-date the critical estuary pollution act. Their processes leave a waste that severely taxes the estuary's oxygen. Oil is also released in small quantities.

Some relief is expected when Burmah connect some (though not all) waste pipes to a local sewage works. Shell have been constructing a pilot plant at the Stanlow refinery to treat their waste biologically but the company said in 1971 that it would be some time before the refinery's effluent is of uniformly high standards. Antony Buckley needs heavy investments, not only from Shell. A number of companies are obliging, such as Laporte Industries at Widnes, which has completed a treatment plant; or Albright & Wilson of Bromborough, who have invested about £20,000 on a plant to remove a high zinc content from their effluent. Or Unilever's Food Industries' factory at Bromborough Port, where a new plant to cut down on fatty waste is being built; or soap makers Joseph Crossfield's of Warrington, who will be connecting trade waste to the local-authority sewer. Some companies, like Vauxhall, have already fulfilled their obligations and discharge a high standard of waste.

Yet laggards survive around the estuary. Widnes industry has 'few positive measures for improvement'[38] at even the design stage – and the principal Widnes companies are I.C.I. Limited, two Fisons factories, Albright & Wilson and Croda International. If the Mersey Estuary is to be substantially improved by 1980, Buckley considers that Widnes industry will have to build the plant to halve its pollution load by 1975, and have full treatment by 1980. Bebington's food industries will have to conquer their fat-waste problems by 1975; Warrington companies, including Thames Board Mills, must have methods to settle waste by 1974 and fully treat it by 1980.

A new, clean Mersey Estuary will cost huge sums. 'Scores of millions of pounds' was an understandably vague estimate proffered by Eldon Griffiths, Under-Secretary of State at the Department of the Environment in July 1971. The government has been attending meetings with the Mersey polluters – especially the local authorities – and has pledged itself to overseeing such a restoration programme. Just one local authority such as Widnes will have to spend £2,500,000 to clean its sewage effluent. A new pumping station, two new sewage works and re-sewering of the central western and southern industrial areas is needed. What Liverpool Corporation's bill will be hardly bears thinking of. The Department of the Environment started in 1971 to collect technical data to arrive at a more precise estimate than Eldon Griffiths'. It may well exceed £100 million.

Yet this price is only the cost that industry and towns now externalize and hand over to the environment. The Mersey Estuary in fact provides an excellent example of how pollution damages an asset. The fisheries in the estuary have declined out of sight, which you would expect. What is surprising about the Mersey is that it has been proved that the pollution actually ensures that it is very hard for the effluent to leave the country. It traps itself within the system. And this trapping very probably adds to the silting up of the estuary, the limitation of its use for shipping and the expense of dredging.

38. Mersey Estuary Report, Table D.

This evidence[39] was provided by two researchers in 1967 – one was John Croft, then biologist with the Lancashire and Western Sea Fisheries Joint Committee, the other was B. A. O'Connor of Liverpool University. Croft and O'Connor knew before they started their working programme that the estuary water contained fine, tiny suspended solids partly composed of organic material from sewage. In fact, the water contains particles called floccules, composed of a core of an inorganic material – a mineral – surrounded by organic material.

Croft and O'Connor proved that much of the sediment on the bottom of the estuary is faeces. This was important, because it was already known that in the Mersey Estuary there is a net landward movement of water near the bed and a net seaward movement at the surface over the tidal cycle. Croft and O'Connor realized that if sediment in suspension was being carried near the bottom, it would thus have trouble in ever leaving the estuary. These suspended solids thus wash up and down the length of the estuary without ever leaving the system. What goes in stays in. The domestic and industrial effluents stick in the estuary. Accordingly Croft and O'Connor predicted that the estuary will deteriorate yet further.

They also thought it would be more likely to silt up – and for a major port like Liverpool, silting is the gravest threat. The sewage would tend to bind with the sand coming into the estuary and make it hard for the sand to be eroded by the effect of the tides. And thus probably the heavy cost of running dredgers, borne by the Mersey Docks and Harbour Board is partly due to the local authorities' failure to pay for anti-pollution controls and to the industrialists putting effluent into the estuary. The 1970 Mersey dredging bill was a cool £1 million.

39. *Effluent and Water Treatment Journal*, Vol. 7, No. 7, pp. 365–74.

Chapter 3

The Frail Sea

In the long, fine summer of 1969 a fisherman of the Scottish Isle of Cumbrae, who makes his living from the deep waters of the Clyde Estuary, noticed something different about the seabirds. One day, as the path of his boat lay across a raft of guillemots floating on the open water, these shy seabirds did not fly off as he approached. They allowed him to come unusually close; they appeared half tame. The first time it happened, the fisherman quickly forgot it; but then it happened again, and then again.

At about the same time, in the month of July, near Fort William – further to the north – birdwatcher Mr J. A. S. Newman recorded that large numbers of guillemots had appeared in Loch Linnhe and Loch Eil. This was also odd: guillemots normally keep clear of inland waters, preferring the coast or the open sea. Mr Newman reported the fact to a naturalist society.

Then, a dying guillemot was found on the other side of the Irish Sea – in Strangford Lough, Northern Ireland. That was at the end of August. Within two weeks amateur naturalists reported seeing groups of guillemots swimming high up in Belfast Lough and other inland waters of Ulster; some said the birds looked poorly. On 5 September, naturalist Mr A. Irvine found ten dead guillemots in Strangford Lough; in the following week he found another fourteen dead birds and by 14 September at least fifty-three dead birds had been reported by naturalists in Ireland.

More and more reports came in of birds washed up dead or coming ashore weak but alive, then dying soon afterwards. Naturalists in Wales reported the first sick bird on this coast on 21 September, and as the wind changed to the west and reached gale force at times, 'scores' of guillemots were driven on to the western coast of Scotland. The local Scottish Society for Prevention of Cruelty to Animals inspector on the Ayrshire coast was deluged with dying birds. He received 656 birds in the last week of September, 400 of which had to be killed at once as beyond help.

Then on 27-8 September the winds rose, gusting to over sixty knots at times and brought on this same Ayrshire coast a cargo of dead and dying birds – some 6,000 in the two days.

Naturalists in different parts of the United Kingdom independently made the same observations: that the guillemots were either waterlogged and unusually tame, or when they were swimming they carried their heads in an unusually low position 'dibbling' their bills in the water. R.S.P.C.A. officers who picked up live guillemots near Liverpool described them as waterlogged and listless; their movements were slow and feeble and their plumage lustreless. One man walked the shore on the south-west of Anglesey during a rising gale at the end of September; he observed large numbers of guillemots coming ashore all 'alive and clean but not very fat and dying within half to one hour, even when placed in shelter'.[1] This was the pattern, broken only by the first 1,500 birds that came ashore on the Clyde; observers saw the guillemots and razorbills there having 'twitches' or rigors – convulsive movements before they died. Common to almost all the reports was one fact: the birds appeared to be exhausted.

These events were the beginnings and the climax of the worst seabird disaster in our history – the Seabird Wreck of 1969, to give the title of the official report it occasioned. By the time it had run its course by early November of that year, between 50,000 and 100,000 seabirds – mainly guillemots – had died. What was and is today alarming about the wreck is not only its casualties – though another mortality on this scale could reduce the guillemot to near rarity on the British coasts – but the causes of deaths. Seriously implicated in the deaths is the contamination of the sea and its natural life by industrial chemicals and metals. In short, it was proved that the sea has become damaged – perhaps irreversibly – and that its natural value and wealth is now grievously at risk. And nowhere is this more true than the seas around Britain. We have seldom been reticent to laying claim to being one of the greater maritime nations in history; the same absence of reticence is needed in venting the newer, less glorious maritime happenings.

1. Report on the Seabird Wreck in the Irish Sea, 1969. Natural Environment Research Council, 1971.

When each tide that autumn in 1969 brought a burden of waterlogged auks, naturalists, amateur and professional, reacted. Corpses were gathered and sent to laboratories for examination. In October researchers at the Nature Conservancy's Experimental Research Station at Monks Wood, near Huntingdon, stumbled on a fact that alarmed and surprised them: the livers of the dead birds had unexpectedly high residues of a family of synthetic industrial chemicals known as P.C.B.s or polychlorinated biphenyls. A wide-scale programme of collection and study was at once launched. From that moment P.C.B.s joined the company of D.D.T. and other persistent pesticides like dieldrin as the enemy of ecosystems in general and organisms in particular.

Indeed P.C.B.s have aspects in common with the notorious organochlorine pesticides, though they are not pesticides themselves. But, like D.D.T., dieldrin and company, P.C.B.s are toxic, persistent – they do not break down into constituent parts easily – and they do build up in the fatty tissue of creatures. And like the organochlorines, they do travel along food chains, concentrating as they go. Thus aquatic plants may well contain minute amounts of P.C.B. and/or D.D.T. but the animals that feed on these plants may build up amounts of several times – perhaps hundreds of times – the concentrations in the plants. The fish that feed on the plant-eating animals concentrate the dose further, the birds that feed on the fish, yet further. Sometimes the dose that seabirds can acquire will kill them.

P.C.B.s are very pervasive. They are used in industry in many different applications, but especially in paints and varnishes, in plastics and as an excellent insulator or coolant in electrical apparatus such as transformers. They escape into the environment in many ways, mainly down the drains. They also reach the sea carried by our rivers from the factory outfalls upstream. Sometimes, as when they are used in marine paints, they are in direct contact with the clean environment, but they have reached the sea, together with a worrying proportion of dangerous heavy metals like lead and cadmium, especially through the agencies of the Greater London Council, Glasgow Corporation and Manchester Corporation. They may have travelled also in the cargoes of some special 'effluent ships' which specialize in disposing of difficult materials. This sea-dumping is one major way in which the marine ecosystem is being threatened.

European dumping is a growth market. A Belgian shipping company, Ahlers, has been reported as converting a double-hulled merchant vessel to dump 100,000 tons a year of titanium dioxide wastes from chemical plants in Belgium.[2] British companies, as we shall see, have been making similar investments. The Netherlands in 1968 was discharging 3,600 tons of sulphuric acid and 750,000 tons a year of sulphur dioxide in the North Sea; West Germany in 1968 was using sea disposal for 375 tons of sulphuric acid a day, 750 tons of iron sulphate a day, 200,000 tons of gypsum a year, 40 tons a month of chlorinated hydrocarbons and 40–50 tons per month of polyethylene.[3] Since 1968 the trade has picked up rapidly. The Dutch government has estimated that in 1968 the total of waste acids dumped in the North Sea was 135,000 tons, and the total of alkalis 4,100 tons. In 1969 the figures rose to 360,000 tons of acids and 12,500 tons of alkalis. In 1970, the figures were 490,000 tons of acids and 23,500 tons of alkalis. Until recently, as Tony Loftas of *New Scientist* commented, there was 'little other than public opinion to stand in the way of the potential ocean dumper'. But in February 1972, the government was one of twelve signatories to a 'Convention for the Prevention of Marine Pollution by Dumping from Ships and Aircraft'. The convention is intended to safeguard the high seas and the territorial waters in the north-east Atlantic region, including the North Sea and part of the Arctic Ocean. Along with Belgium, Denmark, France, West Germany, Finland, Iceland, the Netherlands, Norway, Portugal, Spain and Sweden, Britain will have to regulate all forms of dumping. Undoubtedly the dumping of some toxic substances will be banned altogether.

But this praiseworthy convention does not completely solve the problem. For one thing, parliamentary legislation to put the bans into effect will have to be introduced into each national parliament; this will take time. For another, certain seas are

2. *Chemical Week*, Vol. 109, p. 24.
3. International Council on Exploration of the Sea Report, 1968.

excluded, like the Baltic and the Mediterranean. For a third, it is almost certain that sewage sludges, containing the traces of heavy metals, will be allowed dumping permission, together with other substances, which may or may not be harmless.

But I put the case of P.C.B.s under the microscope first because it shows most clearly the dangers of dumping. What happens is that P.C.B.s used in an industrial process escape into the factory effluent. If this effluent is particularly difficult, it will be collected by one of a number of waste disposal companies. These companies have special tanker ships which take out the liquid waste to authorized dumping grounds.

But very often the factory effluent – containing P.C.B.s and metal traces – goes to the local-authority sewage works. Local authorities have been keen on this idea, because they know that their sewage workers are often more efficient than a private firm's staff. The factory effluent is then treated in the works along with the household and domestic waste. At the end of the process the local authority is left with a semi-liquid sludge, the rest of the water having been purified and returned to the river. Without using up all the river's oxygen and provoking a riot among anglers the sludge certainly cannot be returned to the river. Some of the large authorities – like London, Glasgow, Manchester – ship the sludge out to the dumping grounds. It is this sludge that contains traces of P.C.B.s and heavy metals.

Sludge dumping is thoroughly bad ecological practice. As a rule of thumb, you can say that material that by its nature is hard to dispose of on land will be no less harmful if disposed of in the sea. This was recognized by President Nixon's alert three-man Council on Environmental Quality; in October 1970 the council urged that 'ocean dumping of undigested sewage sludge should be stopped as soon as possible and no new sources allowed' and 'ocean dumping of digested or other stabilized sludge' – the cargo of Glasgow, Manchester, Bristol, Southampton and London – 'should be phased out and no new sources allowed'.

This side of the Atlantic, London relies increasingly on a fleet of 'sludge vessels' which sail twice daily fifty-five miles out into the Thames Estuary to the Barrow Deep dumping ground. The Greater London Council exhibits a certain civic pride in the operation: a council handbook says, 'In a year the mileage steamed would encircle the earth seven times and over three million tons of sludge are disposed of.'[4] Flagship of the fleet is the S.S. *Sir Joseph Bazalgette,* probably the largest sludge ship in Europe, and commemorating the memory of the Sir Joseph who built much of London's sewer network. The *Sir Joseph* sails from either the Beckton or the Crossness sewage works – the two principal treatment centres for central London's waste.

Glasgow shifts its sludge with two ships, the S.S. *Shieldhall* and the larger S.S. *Dalmarnock,* which takes a cargo of 3,500 tons of sludge. With a degree of Scots logic, the S.S. *Dalmarnock* sails from Shieldhall, and the S.S. *Shieldhall* sails from Dramuir, a sewage-treatment works to the west of the city. No doubt it would sail from Dalmarnock, but as that works is some way inland it cannot. The two ships make two trips a day, five days a week, through the Firth of Clyde down to a point six miles south of the Isle of Bute, where the valves are opened and in a period of ten minutes the sludge is off-loaded. In a year about one million wet tons are thus dumped (see map on page 65).

Manchester and Salford run their sludge in ships down the famous Manchester Ship Canal, and out to a dumping ground fanning out from the Bar Light in the Irish Sea. Three ships – the *Percy Dawson,* the *Mancunian,* and the *Salford City* – civic pride again – sail from wharves near the massive Davyhulme sewage works.

These are the three principal public dumpers; they are joined by private enterprise, which handles the industrial effluent too tricky to be sent to local-authority sewage works. In 1971 the market belonged to two or three companies, two of them operating in the North-West. Operating from the Garston Docks near Liverpool's Speke Airport and also from a small dock, Glasson, in North Lancashire, near the town of Lancaster itself, is a subsidiary of Purle, the large disposal company. This is Marine Disposals Ltd, managed until recently by biologist John Croft.

The company runs one vessel, the 349-ton *Marine Seaway,* which shifts (in 1971) about 900 tons a week out of Garston and

4. Over five million tons were disposed of in 1971.

▲ Firth of Clyde: Glasgow Corporation – sludge
〇 Morecambe Bay: Effluent Services/Marine Disposals – trade effluent
△ Liverpool Bay: Manchester/Salford–sludge. Effluent Services/Marine Disposals
— trade effluent
■ Barrow Deep: Greater London Council –sludge
□ Kentish Knock: John Hudson Ltd –plan for trade effluent
● Silver Pit : trade waste
◆ Southampton Corporation–sludge
◇ Bristol Channel. Bristol Corporation–sludge

about 450 tons from Glasson. Running from Glasson, which it does once a week, the *Marine Seaway* proceeds out to a circular dumping area based on a five mile radius around the Morecambe Bay lightship (see map). Running twice a week from Garston, the ship travels to the same dumping ground as used by the Manchester and Salford sludge ships – the triangle fanning out from the Bar Light. Unlike the sludge ships – which tend to open valves or bottom doors and DUMP – the *Marine Seaway* takes five or six hours to dispose of its cargo, cruising slowly around the dumping ground, off-loading at not more than 100 tons an hour through pipes twelve feet under the sea.

Also mixing it with the municipal boats on the Bar Light is the S.S. *Kinder*, once the S.S. *Anthony M* and once a submarine-supply boat. It is based at the Herculeum Dock (1971) in the Port of Liverpool, and runs for its owners – Effluent Services of Stockport – more than 3,000 tons a week of tricky effluent. Like the *Marine Seaway* the *Kinder* does not dump; it disposes, pumping away slowly over a matter of hours.

These north-west disposers have been busy since the late sixties, but 1971 saw a London service proposed to be run by John Hudson with a high target of 400,000 tons a year, a service that at once became the centre of an international row. Indeed, the idea of the *Hudson Stream* on a dumping run from Dagenham to the outer Thames Estuary focused criticism on the activity of dumping. It brought from the Scandinavian countries a renewed determination to get the international agreement to control dumping in the North Sea. It also got valuable publicity for the fears of marine ecologists about dumping – fears that dumping threatens sea and its creatures.

Ecologists such as Dr Kurt Grasshoff, Professor of Marine Chemistry at Kiel University and Dr Karsten Palmörk of the Institute of Marine Research, Bergen, Norway, argue that the activities of all dumpers and disposers are in some aspects objectionable and in the long run liable to cause damage to the marine environment. The Greater London Council's dumping might at first inspection be thought safe; since 1967 the council has used Barrow Deep, which is washed by vigorous tidal action. Tests have shown that the sludge has not deoxygenated the water as has the dumping in the New York Bight, which has worried U.S. authorities so much. Work by the Fisheries Laboratory of the Ministry of Agriculture, Fisheries and Food, at Burnham-on-Crouch in Essex, indicated that even near the bottom of the estuary the oxygen levels were close to full saturation.

But researcher R. G. J. Shelton also found significant quantities of heavy metals, dangerous to many organisms, in both the sludge and the mud of the estuary. In fact more than 1,000 tons of metals like lead, cadmium, zinc, nickel and copper are being dumped by the G.L.C.'s sludge ships every year. We shall see the dangers of such metals later.

Heavy metals are also entering the sea from Manchester and Salford's ships, and from Glasgow's. Assuming the metals are present in roughly the same concentration as in the London sludge, we can assume, on a pro rata basis, that the Irish Sea and the Firth of Clyde are receiving about 200 tons of the metal per year.

But metals are only part of the industrial contribution; also in the package have been traces of organochloride pesticides and P.C.B.s. The sludge ships have been conveying a few ounces of P.C.B. residue with each sailing; over the year this has mounted. Scientists at the Freshwater Fisheries Laboratory at Pitlochry in Scotland analysed fifteen samples of Glaswegian sludge and found P.C.B.s present ranging from 0·1 part per million to the very high concentration of 14 parts per million. On this basis, Dr Alan Holden of the Laboratory calculated that about one ton a year of P.C.B.s were being dumped in the Firth of Clyde. Extrapolating from the concentrations in the London and Manchester sludge, he concluded those cities were also off-loading into the sea about a ton a year of P.C.B.s. There is no doubt that in this way the municipal ships have been a major cause of P.C.B. contamination of the sea.

Traces of metals were also present in the cargoes of the private dumpers; very probably P.C.B.s were present in some loads. Though samples of the 'private' effluent were tested by the Burnham-on-Crouch Fisheries Laboratory, they were not tested specifically for P.C.B.s. But Mr Peter Woods, head of the Marine Pollution Unit at the laboratory, told me in 1971 'I'd expect them

to be there because they're used by large numbers of industries.'
He added, 'No one is throwing away vast quantities of P.C.B.s –
they're too valuable. And you must remember the really toxic
stuff is not disposed of near the coast – it's packed in drums and
dropped over the edge of the Continental Shelf.'

Even if this were the full picture, it is little comfort to
the sea. The oceans are suffering from long-term and low-level
contamination; it is this that is doing as much damage as the
more spectacular cases of mustard gas bubbling up from drums
dumped during the last war. The seabird wreck report was
greatly concerned that the marine environment was being damaged by the slow build-up of heavy metals and industrial
chemicals. The massive slaughter of the guillemots showed this.
The report, written mainly by Dr Martin Holdgate, was a
brilliant exercise in the interpretation of complex evidence. It
showed that the birds did not die from P.C.B.s alone – healthy
guillemots shot specially for examination were found to contain
as much P.C.B. residue as the birds that died. What happened
was something less simple and more disturbing.

This is what seems to have happened: for some reason the
guillemots in that fine summer, in a broad belt of water along the
east coast of Ireland, came under stress. The stress may have
started because the birds were in moult – an annual flightless
phase when the adult birds shed main-wing feathers. The stress
may have been compounded by storms and a change in their diet.
The birds died starving – though the Natural Environment Research Council laboratories did not know enough about the
guillemot's feeding habits to know why. As the birds fought this
stress, as they struggled to survive, they started to use up their fat
reserves – 'mobilized' them, as the report puts it. And this sub-
cutaneous fat was the main place where P.C.B. residues were
located.

Thus mobilized, the P.C.B.s concentrated in the kidneys and
livers of the birds, certainly damaging them and perhaps
affecting the birds' appetites. Guillemots examined by the Monks
Wood researchers were found to have kidneys damaged in the
same way as those of Bengalese finches poisoned experimentally
with P.C.B. In the last analysis it seems the birds died either of

the P.C.B. poisoning, or the further weakening it caused. In addition some of the birds had very high levels of particular metals – especially mercury, lead, cadmium and also arsenic – and may have been weakened further by these concentrations. Said the report: 'Such observations of high tissue concentrations in predators should alert us to the possibility of hazardous levels of these potentially toxic substances in British inshore waters.'

The shattering fact about the report to many bird lovers was the extent to which P.C.B.s had pervaded the wild life, sick and healthy alike. Holdgate himself was perturbed:

It seems likely that, even if pollutants in the seas around Britain are not yet sufficiently concentrated directly to harm wildlife, they may yet increase the chances that a bird which is under stress from some other cause will die rather than recover. Even a small shift in the balance between life and death could have a significant effect on the balance of whole populations. This is especially so with a species such as the larger auks that lay no more than one egg a year and depend for their survival on the fact that the adults normally live for many years and hence breed many times. At present these species are decreasing in numbers, especially because they are the chief victims of oil pollution, and also for reasons that are less well understood. It would be sad if guillemots and razorbills dwindled so much that they no longer provided a spectacle on our rocky coasts – or even worse followed their relative, the great auk, into extinction.

A stuffed great auk was sold for £9,000 at Sotheby's in 1971.

But our fear should not just be for the guillemots but for ourselves: the behaviour of wild creatures is one of the best indicators of the health of our environment. If the guillemots are sick, then the fish may become sick. One thing is certain: when a hardy species not normally subject to wrecks washes up on our coasts in vast dying tides, and is found to contain dangerous levels of toxic substances, then all is not well with the ocean.

Then how do we keep the sea clean? Monsanto Chemicals, the only British manufacturer of P.C.B.s, proved much more enlightened than most of its fellow chemical companies: in March 1971 it withdrew Aroclor 1254, the P.C.B. product, from any application in which it could escape into the environment – that is, in use like paints and varnishes. No doubt the withdrawal had aspects of self-interest – Monsanto are trying to develop a 'safe' P.C.B. and don't want a government ban on all uses of the product – but none the less the withdrawal must have halved Monsanto's P.C.B. business. The crucial point that will have to be established is whether P.C.B. levels do in fact go down. At least three Western European companies have a P.C.B. trade in Britain – Bayer make P.C.B.s in Germany, Prodelec in France and Flix in Spain. Will these companies also withdraw P.C.B.s from dangerous uses? More crucial still, will the levels in the sludge ships fall to nothing?

Even if these answers prove to be cheering, the real problem remains: the daily round-trips of the low-slung ships, out to the dumping grounds and back. P.C.B.s are only one industrial chemical of many that the future may suddenly find are polluting the environment. Then there are the heavy metals, a threat to our livelihood that the public is only just beginning to appreciate.

The sludges all contain traces of metals, including the toxic lead, chromium and cadmium. This last metal is now being appreciated as a killer. The classic case of cadmium poisoning occurred among middle-aged Japanese women near Toyoma. The rice and soya beans these women ate and cooked was grown in fields irrigated with water from the River Jintsu, which was contaminated with cadmium from mining tips. Since 1962 223 cases of cadmium poisoning in the village have been reported. The symptoms are tiredness, shortness of breath and an impaired sense of smell, caused by decalcification of the skeleton and damage to the kidneys. The poisoning is extremely painful – the Japanese graphically call it 'itai-itai'. Some of the women died.

The levels of contamination in our seas is frightening; in 1968 a working party in the United States looking into metal contamination of shellfish suggested that two parts per million for marketable oysters should be the limit for combined concentrations of four toxic heavy metals (mercury, lead, chromium and cadmium). But in 1972 Dr. Graham Nickless of Bristol University showed that some limpets in the Bristol Channel had average levels of cadmium of 550 parts per million. The source is most probably industrial. The limpets were taken near the Avonmouth estate, and cadmium is associated with zinc smelting. While it is undoubtedly true much of the cadmium ends up in the sea from the natural erosion of cadmium-bearing strata, it is folly to add more cadmium via the sludge ships. In its erratic manner the Ministry of Agriculture decided to survey cadmium levels in the North Sea at the same time as it cooperated in the proposed dumping in that sea by John Hudson's ship.

The five dumping cities will assure you that all is well. London says its dumping site is well washed; Glasgow points out that it dumps into 600 feet of water and that tests have shown dispersal is very good. Manchester and Salford, far from being contrite, are considering taking part in building a new tanker terminal on Merseyside to which sludge would be piped from the two cities and other regional centres. Sludge ships would no longer have to make the fifty-three miles journey along the Manchester Ship Canal, and five times as much sludge could be dumped within the next twenty years.

The trouble is that the whole operation of the cities' sewage works is now hand-in-glove with industry. Apart from really noxious effluents, the sewage works must take the effluents of countless companies; in fact, their sewage departments have agreements with the companies to do so, charging a rate for treatment. The idea was to get the industries to 'send to sewer' rather than have the assistant under works manager of Muck and Brass Limited, Lancashire, turn the wrong wheel and present the river with a fish-killing load. Certainly the improvement in many of Britain's rivers has been due to this policy, but now, it seems that the rivers have been saved at the expense of the sea. The corporations in their ignorance have not been playing the 'ecological game' of Professor Barry Commoner, the American ecologist. This is just to ask continually one question 'Where does it go?' So you ask the Greater London Council about the sewage, and the council says proudly – 'Look at the Thames: the muck doesn't go into the river any more!' Then where does it go? 'Oh, into our specially constructed sludge vessels.' Then where does it go? 'Oh, fifty-five miles out into the Thames Estuary, and dumped into the deep, deep, Barrow Deep.' Then where do the metals and chemicals go? 'Washed away by the tide.' Then where does it go? Where does it go? Where does it go? If the council doesn't answer, ask the creatures of the sea, from the plankton to the penguins.

The solution is appallingly hard to see: massive investments have been made in our existing sewerage system, and in the pipes that take industry's effluent and deliver it to the treatment works. To undo all this – so the human waste can be treated without being contaminated by industrial muck and could thus be safely used for agriculture – will be very difficult. The best way is to try to monitor closely the incoming industrial effluent and force companies with even small loads of dangerous industrial chemicals or metals to remove them first or change their manufacturing process. That is a hard task.

The problems of the private dumping trade were spotlighted in 1971 when two dumping trips became the centre of international disputes. At the eye of the fiercest storm was a small, ageing Dutch tanker, the *Stella Maris*. She was hired in mid 1971 for waste disposal by the world's second largest producer of chemical fibres, the Netherlands-based group Akzo Zout Chemie. The cargo was 600 tons of chlorinated aliphatic hydrocarbons, a waste from the manufacture of P.V.C. On the advice of two Dutch government scientific institutes, A.K.Z.O. directed the *Stella Maris* to dump it off the Norwegian coast, at a point where the sea is around 6,000 feet deep.

A more controversial dumping ground could not have been chosen. Not only are the Norwegians more conscious than any other nation in the world of the damage dumping can do to sea fishing, but their scientists were especially alarmed at research results into precisely the cargo that the *Stella Maris* had on board. A quantity of chlorinated aliphatic hydrocarbon waste had been dumped in 1970 and the results monitored by the Norwegian researcher *Johan Hjort*. The results were published in a paper produced by Norwegian and Swedish scientists at the F.A.O. Technical Conference in December 1970 on Marine Pollution. The first report from the *Johan Hjort* indicated that chlorinated aliphatic hydrocarbon was not the innocuous cargo many had assumed. The ship reported: 'High densities of particles were observed, and within some areas the sea was coloured red-white by the particles ... They looked like dead plankton.' The analysis was confirmed by laboratory checks – the dead plankton were the crustacean *Calanas fin-marchicus* – an important member of the marine foodchain of many commercially important fish.

The Scandinavian scientists found that chlorinated aliphatic hydrocarbons are widely distributed in the North Atlantic, and have originated from both American and European dumpers. Most worrying of all, tests showed that the chemicals seriously hamper the photosynthetic capacity of the plants in the plankton – the first step in the marine foodchain. Then it was discovered that a small proportion of the waste can be extremely persistent, and laboratory experiments indicated that young plaice and cod are extremely susceptible.

So when the *Stella Maris* left Rotterdam on 15 July and set course towards Norway, it only needed news of her cargo to leak out for an uproar to break out. This happened before the *Stella Maris* had even passed the German coast – A.K.Z.O. do not know the source of the leak – and immediately the Dutch Ministry of Foreign Affairs had objections on its desk from the Danish and Norwegian Governments. When the *Stella Maris* reached the dumping ground, it was ordered to wait; then A.K.Z.O. – on the advice of the two Dutch scientific institutes again – fixed a dumping ground about 625 miles north-west of Ireland and the same distance south of Iceland at a 9,000 feet depth. But then objections came from the Irish, the British (even) and Icelandic governments. But these complaints were only the beginning of the ordeal the *Stella Maris* had to bear. Running out of fresh meat and vegetables for the much longer voyage, the ship decided to pull into Thorshavn in the Faeroe Islands. The natives, who depend upon fishing for their living, were extremely unfriendly. On the quayside 400 demonstrators were waiting; on the water long-boats crewed by tough fishermen rowed up and down the quay to prevent the ship berthing; in the water frogmen swam bearing protest placards aloft. The *Stella Maris* was driven off, and the captain turned south, aiming for Stornoway in the Hebrides, where he hoped he could pick up both fuel and food.

Remarkably, however, the British Government ordered the Stornoway harbour authorities not to fuel or aid the ship. Once again, the *Stella Maris* changed course.

As she headed now for Ireland, the directors of A.K.Z.O. heard increasingly alarming reports. Three Irish minesweepers stood by to intercept the ship if she entered Irish waters; the Irish Republican Army, that most excitable handler of explosives, was said to be planning to destroy the ship if she came into Belfast for fuel or food, or alternatively to attack A.K.Z.O. subsidiaries in Ireland. (A.K.Z.O. owns sixty-two per cent of British Enkalon, which has a large synthetic fibre plant on Antrim, and is establishing a £20 million steel-cord factory near Limerick.) After a board meeting, the directors ordered the *Stella Maris*'s owners to recall her, complete with cargo, to Rotterdam. On the sultry evening of 25 July, the *Stella Maris*, her name painted over, approached the entrance to Rotterdam. But she turned tail rapidly when journalists and photographers sailed out to meet her. Only after dark did the ship enter and tie up. Wives and mothers waited on the quayside and clambered aboard as the gang-plank came down. Reporters were repelled. A month later, the *Stella Maris* was no more. The ship was re-named *Constance*.

The *Stella Maris* affair showed the British authorities in an enlightened mood. This attitude was less apparent in the international dispute which broke out when it was learnt that John Hudson's waste-disposal division proposed to dump with the *Hudson Stream*. The real importance of this ship is this: it is custom-built, especially for dumping. With four huge tanks and special hydraulic equipment to unload, her master, Captain Peter Mallows could tell me with pride: 'This ship is so good I can dump 1,500 tons in five minutes. You can see the ship come up out of the water.' The other British dumping ships, with the exception of the municipal sludge ships, have been adapted from craft lent to many trades. But John Hudson paid about £500,000 to the Dutch shipbuilders Vuyk & Zonen of Capelle a/d Ijssel for the *Hudson Stream,* and had her fitted with the most modern navigational and disposal equipment available.

Hudson Stream's size is one further difference from the other dumper ships. She can carry and dispose of in a day almost as much as the *Marine Seaway* (of Marine Disposals Limited) can manage in a week. In a full year she may dump as much as 500,000 tons or about one ninth the total amount of industrial waste dumped by the United States in 1968. Planned to operate from Dagenham Dock, just behind the Ford factory, the *Hudson Stream* would dump British waste near the Kentish Knock, a point in the outer Thames Estuary (see map) but she was designed for a fully European business. John Hudson employees negotiated contracts to collect industrial waste from companies in France, Belgium, Holland and Germany. The low draught of the ship is a design feature to allow it to penetrate the major rivers, such as the Trent and the Rhine, to collect the chemical waste from inland companies.

The *Hudson Stream* was launched with more than the 15 × 5 miles Thames Estuary dumping ground in mind. It was built to use the Continental disposal ways also – the dumping ground off the Belgian coast; the Dutch method by which a dumping ship is required to steam at a certain speed away from the Dutch coast at right angles; and the German dumping ground near Heligoland. The ship, in fact, marked the arrival of sea dumping in Europe as an integral part of industrial production. Land-disposal sites are becoming harder and harder to find because of objections of the people who have to live near them and fear of the water authorities that leaching of the effluent may contaminate water supplies. So everyone has turned to the sea. The sea has these great attractions for dumpers: for long, it has been beyond the law. You can dump anything except oil outside the three-mile limit and be safe from prosecution. Outside the limit is outside the law, at least until the anti-dumping convention is ratified by European parliaments. Out at sea there are no residents (except the silent fish) to protest at a spoilt amenity and there are fewer officials present to peer and probe.

The *Hudson Stream* case provoked all the Scandinavian countries to ask all other countries with fishing interests in the North Sea to agree to control industrial-waste dumping in fishing waters. Iceland, Sweden, Norway, Finland and Denmark also started to push ahead with legislation to prevent their own companies from dumping.[5]

The British have been schizophrenic about dumping with officials both enlightened and reactionary. Mr Peter Walker, Secretary of State to the Department of the Environment, said in an interview with the *Observer* published in May 1971 that he was very worried about the effect of industrial dumping and would like to see international control. And the pollution watchdog, the Royal Commission on Environmental Pollution, said in its first report (published February 1971) that urgent action was needed on the disposal of noxious wastes at sea.

On the other hand, Britain is also represented by the Ministry of Agriculture, Fisheries and Food, at times a most obscurantist and backwoods department, confident in technology, optimistic that pollution is nothing really to worry about. Time and again I have been told that practice Y or product X was quite safe 'provided it is controlled in our manner' and then watched to see Y or X withdrawn in countries around the world, and finally proving so objectionable that even Britain has changed its policy though not without some obstinate rearguard actions from the Ministry. Thus when finally Britain realized that D.D.T. and the organochlorine pesticides were a major danger to the environment (after long campaigns by scientists like Dr Kenneth Mellanby and Dr Norman Moore), the Government accepted advice and banned the most toxic organochlorines for most practices, and also withdrew D.D.T. from garden use, on the correct grounds that there were perfectly good alternatives on the market which did not threaten to pole-axe wildlife.

It fell to the Ministry of Agriculture to implement this ban, which it did with singular ill-grace and marked inefficiency. Thus late in 1970 it allowed British companies, who had already profited greatly from marketing these pesticides, a stay of execution on the date the chemicals had to be withdrawn from the market. They were given another nine months in which to clear

5. International repercussion in fact halted the initial dumping programme of the *Hudson Stream*. Planned to start dumping in March, by November the ship was still lying idle at Dagenham. Financial losses, say John Hudson, were caused by this postponement.

their stocks. Manufacturers went to the Ministry of Agriculture and pointed out that by the time the ban came along they would not have sold all the little cartons and plastic packets to gardeners. It was only the *containers* the companies were worried about, since D.D.T. was retained for other non-garden uses. The Ministry granted this further period which increased the contamination of living things and even continued to market a booklet called *Chemicals for the Gardener* which advocated D.D.T. for uses the Government had already banned. When I asked the Ministry about this, a spokesman told me that the booklet in fact facilitated the ban, since it encouraged gardeners to buy D.D.T. products, thus using up the stocks and hastening the time when D.D.T. could be banned and prevented from causing damage to the environment. The spokesman's words appeared suitably in the *New Statesman*'s 'This England' column, repository for the screwball utterances of Englishmen.

The Ministry has been as unenlightened about the sea as it has about the land. On dumping its policy has caused the minimum of real control and the maximum of public deception. Over and over again obscurantists in Whitehall have made policy from their own prejudices; the views of the Ministry's own excellent scientists at their fisheries laboratories have not been paramount. The Ministry has perpetrated a fiction that 'low concentrations of toxic materials are dispersed and do no damage'. It was doing just that in 1971, a decade after Rachel Carson showed just how death-dealing low concentrations could be.

The control method of industrial dumping, both of the private companies and the Ministry of Agriculture, is well illustrated by the John Hudson system. To be fair to the company, it *wanted* to do its business safely; when I first made inquiries about its planned dumping, I was given all the help I needed, and my inquiries were courteously answered by John Belcher, the chief executive of John Hudson's waste-disposal division. He and his consultant chemist, Dr S. H. Jenkins, outlined this control system:

1. The customer has to complete a detailed control form, which requires a full description of the manufacturing process from which the waste is derived, its chemical composition, and

which specifically asks the client to state both the amount of certain chemicals which may be present and to guarantee the absence of other chemicals – organochlorines, P.C.B.s, arsenicals – which Hudson declare they will not handle.

2. The client company is then asked to provide a sample of the effluent, which is then analysed by Hudson's consultant chemists, Bostock Hill & Rigby, a reputable Birmingham company that works both for private companies and for public authorities.

3. A written description of Bostock Hill & Rigby's analysis is then sent to the Marine Pollution Laboratory, part of the Ministry's fisheries laboratory at Burnham-on-Crouch. Scientists there tell Hudson whether the material can be dumped. B.H.R. then tell staff down at Dagenham Dock how to make up the *Hudson Stream*'s cargo, so that two incompatible substances will not be mixed. Hudson's policy is to dilute any material to one tenth of its toxic concentration, reckoning the actual discharge will dilute it a further hundredfold.

4. The exact place and time of the dumping is noted; it is claimed that slow discharge rates are used for certain substances; Ministry officials are encouraged to make checks to see that there is no harm to the marine environment, using tracer dyes if necessary to see the pattern of dispersion.

With variations, this has been the set pattern of 'voluntary' dumping control. How good is it? Well, it is far from safe and the blame lies not so much with the dumpers as with the Ministry. For one thing, the sample of effluent Hudson's and the other private dumpers require of the client company is usually provided by the company itself. How can Hudson's *et al.* be sure that the sample represents actually the make-up of any load they are required to dump? A 'representative' sample would have to be made up of a collection of small samples taken over at least a twenty-four hour period – or the length of the manufacturing process. Effluents change wildly in some industries, swinging from extreme acidity to extreme alkalinity. How can a dumper take into account from a sample the possibility that a workman will tip a solution of P.C.B.s into a waste collection tank? It won't show on the questionnaire; it won't show in the sample; it won't show in the description sent to Burnham-on-Crouch; it will show in the carcass of a seabird.

With sloppy methodology, the Ministry of Agriculture do not test each sample of effluent itself; the Burnham-on-Crouch scientists do it occasionally. 'Three times a year or so' was an estimation given to me in 1971 by Burnham-on-Crouch. Even on the rare occasions they do test, they have been doing so cavalierly; thus in 1971 the Ministry scientists were not testing for P.C.B.s, though at the time the damage P.C.B.s were suspected of causing was very well known.

If pressed, the scientists will admit they do not know for certain what is being dumped. 'We can't check every road tanker load. There is a risk that one load will not be the same as another,' said Dr J. E. Portman of the Marine Pollution Unit at Burnham-on-Crouch. By the same token they don't know exactly what has been going into the *Kinder* run by Effluent Services; or the *Marine Seaway* of Marine Disposal. Nor in 1971 did companies. Ian Holland, managing director of Effluent Services, told me he'd *like* to know just what an individual shipload was composed of but 'at the moment you'd have to analyse a fairly large number of samples and that is not very practicable'. John Croft, the manager of Marine Disposals, was very frank:

We try to test ten per cent of our loads. But the results can take fourteen days to come through, by which time we've disposed of the load. If the analysis reveals a potentially damaging substance, the only thing we can do then is to attack the company that sent it. It's a little frail. We are very much at the mercy of the companies bringing stuff to us.

The principle of allowing dumping (much repeated by Ministry spokesmen) is based on the philosophy of the 'immensity of the sea' – the same sort of feeling that motivates second-rate poets when confronted with a liquid horizon. 'Dilution' is their key word – if anything is dilute enough, they tell you, all's well. And up to a point they are quite right. Trouble is, more and more evidence is coming up which shows the appalling damage done by a fraction of a few parts per million. Thus endosulfan, the pesticide chemical that was one suspect in the killing of the Rhine fish population in 1969, is toxic to fresh-water fish at minute concentrations – one part per thousand million. The Ministry men are obsessed with death, perhaps because it always causes their telephones to ring with complaints from the public. They worry most about toxicity – about fish leaping out of the water in death spasm. The more gradual break-up of an ecosystem, less spectacular, concerns them less.

Yet it just may be the gradual invasion of the environment by small quantities of toxic or even non-toxic substances that is its undoing. Dr Karsten Palmörk, of the Institute of Marine Research, Bergen, Norway, believes that the dumping in the North Sea may have 'disastrous' effects on the marine life because of the pheronome factor. Pheronomes are excretions given out by fish in minute quantities, under a few parts per *billion,* which act as sex attractants, guides to feeding grounds, assisting the homing instinct – a number of vital purposes. Palmörk believes the pheronomes may not survive in a sea solution also containing small quantities of industrial waste. The dreadful thing about this is that we won't know for certain until it is too late to reverse the effect.

If the Ministry of Agriculture is jumpy about highly toxic substances in Britain's immediate waters, it has had an easier conscience about the deeper sea. It sanctions – it cannot forbid – the dumping of drums of highly toxic materials – like pesticides and mercury – over the edge of the Continental Shelf. The fantastic growth of the chemical industry has given a massive disposal problem. The Ministry's policy is to persuade firms to contract with a shipping firm to dump the stuff in drums. This is absolutely safe, it says. Then, putting its foot in its mouth, it refuses to tell the public where the dumping sites are, or what is dumped by whom.

The Norwegians, however, spurred by complaints of their fishermen that they were trawling as many as eight barrels of highly toxic material a day, probed further into the drum dumping. Dr Palmörk and his colleagues G. Berge and R. Ljoen first of all examined some of the drums trawled up. One contained 'a black tarry substance of hydrocarbons' originating from the themoplastic industry, and quite toxic. With clever detective work, the Norwegians examined the stones in the concrete used to weigh the drums. From these, they were able to say the drums originated from the Main or Weser areas in Germany.

Then, with the help of two journalists, the scientists tried to piece together how much was being dumped by whom. They discovered a number of dumpers, including one company which admitted it had probably dumped 10,000 drums. They also found out the dumping procedure: the drums were taken by a contractor to a ship broker. The broker found a ship travelling near the dumping site, agreed a contract, and asked for a copy of the ship's log when the journey had been completed, to show where the drums had gone overboard.

This, at least, was the practice in theory. In fact, it seems that many captains get impatient with the drums taking up space and heave them over the side as soon as their ship disappears over the horizon. A great many of the drums have been trawled up by fishermen many miles south of the dumping area known to the Norwegians.

The Norwegian scientists comprehensively demolished the arguments for dumping. They pointed out that most of the area is fished with bottom trawlers and it doesn't help fishing if the cod come up with a couple of hundredweight of petrochemical waste in a leaking drum. Fishing gear is destroyed and the leaking drums are a threat to the fishermen themselves. Worse, the leaking drums must be damaging the bottom waters, the chemicals being taken by drift into the Skagerrak, the area between Denmark and Norway, and thus destroying the important nursery areas for the fish populations of the North Sea and the Norwegian Sea, destroying plankton and fish larvae. Exactly the same arguments apply to the British dumping.

Actually stopping the dumping, whether it be of drums or liquid sludge or watery waste, is easy enough: the ships can be prevented from leaving port. Solving the disposal problem is harder. Greatly overpopulated Northern Europe is short of land; unlike, say, the U.S.S.R., it lacks large areas of unproductive, unpeopled land where waste lagoons can be constructed. We shall probably have to look to technology to solve the problem, perhaps by near-complete recovery of materials from the waste and the neutralization of other toxic materials. In this way, the heavy metals could be used and re-used.

However, the dumping problem will be easier to solve than the largest threat of all to the sea; oil, the fluid upon which modern industry is based. Britain is too perilously positioned to have much chance of avoiding grievous oil damage – spillages from craft that will make the *Torrey Canyon* look like a bath toy. About 900 ships a day pass through the English Channel and the Strait of Dover, headed for Britain, for Europoort, for Germany and Scandinavia. Many of these ships are oil tankers and there is one trend in tankers: they're getting larger. When, on 18 March 1967, the *Torrey Canyon*, with a clear day, calm water and insurance rating 100A1 from Lloyds ran straight into the Seven Stones, she was the thirteenth largest ship in the world. Her tonnage was 120,000 dead weight tons; by February 1971 more than 100 tankers were over 200,000 d.w.t., with a further 250 under construction. One of these tankers was 376,000 d.w.t., three times the *Torrey Canyon*. The Japanese, obsessed with notions of growth, are building two 477,000 d.w.t. tankers, the first for delivery in 1973. According to a shipping expert, Commander Michael Ranken, the first million-ton tanker will be built before the end of the decade, unless it is legally prevented.

The motive of the oil companies is obvious. Massive economy can be made by shipping in bulk. The truth is also that this money is made at someone else's expense: it's another 'externalized cost'. The oil companies gain in cheaper freight costs; citizens and creatures pay as Kuwait crude floats on the sea, chokes the auks, kills the fish, fouls the beaches.

The hazard differs from dumping in that it comes about by accident: the slow crunch as two tankers, half a mile apart, cannot avoid collision. (It takes a 250,000 tanker more than three miles to stop from moderate speed.) Of all waters, the seas around Britain are appallingly ill-suited to such traffic: the Channel and North Sea are shallow waters, covered with sandbanks and areas of shifting sandwaves. Through these banks and waves travel the tankers, with draughts now down to sixty-five feet. Look at any Admiralty chart of the Channel and North Sea, and it is clear how fine the tanker shipping companies are running things. Many of them are passing only a few feet over the sea bottom. They're taking this risk in the following conditions: *knowing* that below ten fathoms (sixty feet) the Admiralty charts cannot totally be relied upon; *knowing* that the water depth can fluctuate six or seven feet according to meteorological conditions; *knowing* that areas have been identified where sandwaves up to fifty feet high appear where they were not known before; *knowing* that a ship at speed tends to 'squat' – to lower itself in the water – by a few feet.

The consequence of running aground is that the tanker can break its back as the level lowers. In mid 1971 the oil companies were worried enough about one shipping route (between the Sandettie and Fairy Bank) to run their tankers on a new route which is deeper but more dangerous in that it means running against the flow of the shipping traffic.

In short, the risks of a massive oil spill and the coming of the time when no seabirds will be left on the shores near a major shipping route are greater and closer with the march of technology. It is estimated that between 150,000 and 450,000 seabirds are killed each year by oil spills in the North Sea and the Atlantic (J. J. C. Jarvis at the Conference on Oil Pollution at Sea; Rome 1968).

But there are a number of expedients that will lessen the chance of a spill (though the best way to ensure a mega-spill does not happen is to switch to an economy that uses less fuel and power). Most of these I draw from an excellent paper by Cmdr Michael Ranken.[6] One necessity is to get ships to behave as aircraft: stick to certain routes and be punished if they leave them. Nowhere in the world is such routing compulsory. In 1967, by voluntary agreement, such routing was put into effect in the Strait of Dover, and Ranken estimates that by 1971, ninety-five per cent of the ships were sticking to the channels. The trouble is that 'five per cent represents forty ships a day', and these ships are protected from prosecution by a piece of maritime mumbo-jumbo known as Rule 29, 'the rule of good seamanship'.

6. *Mandatory Technicological Aids and Traffic Control Essential for All Channel Shipping*, March 1971, Aquamarine International Ltd, London.

Next it will be necessary to make pilots compulsory on all commercial vessels (despite the fact that a pilot was aboard the *Pacific Glory* at the time of the collision with the *Allegro* in 1970). Higher dues must be charged to the ships to pay for the better pilotage. Speed limits, says Ranken, should be imposed in certain sections of the routes, and vessels over a certain draught should be banned from the Strait of Dover and be restricted to west-coast ports like Milford Haven or the Clyde.

Ranken also wants to see better training for watchkeeping officers; some are better at clockwatching. International agreement will be needed to make this effective – regrettable because it will take years to accomplish. Commander Ranken is worried also about the very long stretches officers have to serve at sea; the master of the *Torrey Canyon* had been without leave for a year and two days at the time of the wreck. Six-month stretches are common on the super tankers, since in order to maximize profits the oil companies like to keep them in service for 350 to 355 days a year and give them less than twenty-four hours for turn-around at each loading and discharge. Ranken suggests four months should be a reasonable stretch. Most of all, he would like to see legal jurisdiction in the Channel and the North Sea pushed out from the three-mile limit to the median line between countries on either shore. This jurisdiction already extends to the mining industries – like oil and gas – and the main point of it would be to allow the country being threatened by a maverick master flying a flag of convenience to get redress of the type it wanted.

The real target for control should be to make ships emulate aircraft. An aeroplane flies on a certain route, at a certain height and speed, under the guidance of ground control who know precisely where it is and what it is doing. Computer systems are in service that monitor up to 500 aircraft simultaneously. Ferranti Limited already believe that it would technically be possible to construct such a radar system to guide ships through the Strait of Dover, at a cost of about £2 million, or one seventh the cost of a 250,000-ton tanker. A chain of twenty to thirty radar sites, unmanned, could be constructed to cover the main coastal areas of the English Channel. The sites could be linked by broad-band microwave links to a few area control centres. The same approach would work equally well for other danger channels like the entrance to the Baltic. Captains would speak to shore control in the way pilots talk to ground control, though with no doubt a new nautical flavour. The system might put up the price of petrol slightly; it would lower the social cost of having oil companies. The real cost of an oil-based economy is illustrated by the remarkable fact that the motor car is a major polluter of the world's oceans. This is startling, especially when one remembers that every year about seven per cent of the world's fleet is estimated to be involved in collisions at sea.[7] The influx of oil and oil products into the sea from rivers and seas has been estimated at about 5 million metric tons a year. Shipping operations and accidents add about another one million tons a year. But then motor-vehicle emissions contribute a further 1·8 million tons,[8] 'making automobile crankcases a bigger source of marine pollution than all kinds of marine activity put together'. Worse is to come: by 1980 world production of petroleum is expected to be almost double the 1970 total of 2,200 million metric tons.

7. 'The Sea. Prevention and control of marine pollution.' Report of United Nations Secretary General, 7 May 1971.

8. *Man's Impact on the Global Environment; Assessments and Recommendations for Action.* Massachusetts Institute of Technology Press, 1970.

Chapter 4

Unwanted Sound

One of the barriers the conservation movement yet has to sur-
mount is the eradication of a public impression that it is mostly
concerned with protecting the environment of property owners
from the claims of the dispossessed. There are elements of truth
in the accusation when, for example, it concerns local campaigns
to protect a stretch of coast from the march of the caravan sites
and the low-cost holidays they afford; or when it concerns the
immensely larger issue of the resource piracy of the First World
by the developed countries, that will ensure that most of the
countries of the Third World will be 'never-to-be-developed', in
Paul Ehrlich's phrase. This issue is a potential flash-point in the
relation between the richer and the poorer countries.

But if the term 'environment' is interpreted in a wider sense,
rather than confined to the issues of parks and trout streams, one
thing is obvious: the worst physical environments are inhabited
by the most depressed strata of society, and any conservation
movement worth its name must be pledged to start from the
bottom, from the mean back-to-back terraces or the new vertical
slums of the cheap skyscraper housing blocks. It is the British
working class, obviously enough, who have inherited the most
ravaged environments in this country. The areas where the acreage of derelict land is the highest – Lancashire, Durham, South
Wales, the West Riding of Yorkshire – is where industry has been
centred and the work people to serve those industries have lived.
The highest levels of lead contamination in the blood of British
children are found in urban children, predominantly working
class.

The same is true of air pollution. The Alkali Inspectorate does
most of its work in areas where the housing is poor.

One further species of pollution particularly afflicts the industrial class, yet is peculiar in that though it palpably inflicts great
and measurable damage, it is met with a mixture of fatalism,
indifference and bravado: it is not a cause for concern. Industrial

noise affects and damages many thousands, probably hundreds of thousands, of workers. Prolonged exposure to high noise levels – sound levels above eighty-five decibels on the A scale (dBA)[1] – permanently damages hearing. The jute mills of Dundee afford an example – they have been closely studied because they offer ideal conditions to the researcher. To calculate how occupationally induced deafness is caused, the researcher must locate workers whose degree of deafness can be related to the noise they work in. Too frequently a worker will have been found to have worked on a variety of machines, with differing noise levels, or he may have served in the armed forces, an experience – because of gunfire – that usually damages hearing. But some of the Dundee jute weavers have been working on the same looms for more than fifty years, looms that were installed in the late nineteenth century and are still working today.

The Department of Occupational Medicine at Dundee University has wisely made use of the test-bed on its doorstep. Researchers led by Dr William Taylor found these consequences of industrial noise: a quarter of a sample of workers with long experience of the looms were found to be deaf or part-deaf. The noise in the weaving sheds was found to be so high that of a group of fifty-seven women weavers, sixty-one per cent practised lip-reading. In this same group three quarters of the women said they disliked the telephone or were not able to use it; they said their hearing damage prevented them from discriminating who was speaking to them. About half the women had to take front seats at church or cinema, while nine of them found they could not go to public meetings or entertainments at all. That said, it is none the less true that the Dundee weaving sheds are by no means the noisiest working places in Britain.

They are quiet, for example, compared to the dressing shops of the largest propeller manufacturing unit in the world, the fac-

1. This scale is taken from the weighting of a type of sound-level meter which reduces its reponses to low and very high frequencies so as more nearly to match the response of the human ear. An increase of three decibels represents a doubling in sound-pressure level – which is not the same thing as a doubling in noise as we hear it. The A scale takes account of *perceived* noise levels and the characteristics of the human ear. Thus ten decibels on the A scale account for a doubling in perceived noise.

tory of Stone Manganese Marine, at Wallasey, on the bank of the
Mersey Estuary opposite to Liverpool. Propellers are cast there
as near to design size as possible, the blades often weighing sixty to
eighty tons. The surplus metal on the castings are attacked by
men called trimmers with pneumatic hand chisels, reducing the
metal to the predetermined shape. Prominent irregularities in the
castings are removed by men called fettlers, again using pneumatic hand chisels.

Hearing damage has been inflicted on an employee of Stone
Manganese. This fact was established in 1971 when a South
London worker, fifty-year-old Frank Berry, sued the company
after he worked for fourteen years in what the judge termed 'an
inferno of noise'. The case of *Berry* v. *Stone Manganese Marine*
will prove a crucial judgement, joining precedent-setting cases
in industrial-injury law like *Stokes* v. *G.K.N.*, in which the wife
of a tool-setter was awarded £10,000 damages after her husband
died of scrotal cancer, caused by contact with oil at his workplace.

Frank Berry became in December 1971 the first man to succeed
in court with a common law claim for occupationally induced
deafness. When he joined Stone Manganese and went to work in
the Charlton shop, there was nothing wrong with his hearing. He
worked in the chipping shop on processes including shaping the
manganese-bronze propellers with pneumatic hammers. He told
the judge, Mr Justice Ashworth, that the first day he walked into
the chipping shop, the noise frightened him out of his life.
Another witness described the noise as bordering on the threshold
of pain. Both evidences are understandable when one realizes the
noise level amounted to about 115 and 120 decibels – a noise level
you might hear if you stood with your ear close to the loud-
speakers of a noisy rock group. Over the years Mr Berry's hearing suffered, he found it a handicap some three years after he
joined the company. The judge told him that damages for his
deafness and all the discomfort he had suffered since 1960
merited compensation of about £2,500. But for legal reasons
compensation was awarded only for deterioration since 1967, and
Mr Berry was awarded £1,250.

Close analysis of the hearing of the fettlers and trimmers in
Stone Manganese at Wallasey and in an iron foundry was

undertaken in 1967 by three researchers from the Department of Occupational Health at Manchester, G. R. C. Atherley, W. G. Noble and D. B. Sugden.[2] Since the propeller material is like bell metal, the researchers found first that the men were working in a maximum noise level of between 100 and 115 decibels, levels between two and five times the sound of heavy lorries passing close by in the street. On the older trimmers and fettlers, men in their fifties, the noise appeared to have taken a terrible toll. The sample of trimmers (average age 45·7 years) who had been working more than eighteen years in the plant had a decibel hearing loss of about 68 decibels – or, in other words, had lost about 68 per cent of their hearing ability. The fettlers (average age 53·5) who had worked more than twenty-one years at the works, had a 65 decibel loss. These men were markedly more damaged than other working groups also examined and tested by the researchers for comparison purpose. Thus a group of bus drivers (average age 53·7) was found to have a loss of 44 decibels, printers 35 decibels, cardroom operatives 52 decibels, weavers 58 decibels, boiler makers 55 decibels, and iron moulders 43 decibels. Since hearing naturally declines with age (a process known as presbyacusis), it would be normal for someone in his fifties to have a 30 decibel loss.

The diagram overleaf shows the hearing loss of the foundrymen.

Some foundry workers explained to a B.B.C. nationwide programme broadcast first in 1970 just what hearing loss meant to them. The reporter Philip Tibenham asked one if he had any difficulty in hearing him. The man replied, 'Well, now and again, you see, I just have to sort of lean forward, for the keeping in with the conversation, sort of thing, and to follow your question or spoken word.' Another said, 'When I go home and I'm sitting down, reading the paper, people talk to me in the house, and I just don't hear them, and they put it down to my ignorance. And then they tell me to turn the television down because it's too loud for them, and I can't hear if I don't have it louder.' A third worker said, 'Even if you go for a drink, in conversations you've got to keep saying "Pardon".'

Hearing damage is inflicted chiefly by long and continuous

2. *Annals of Occupational Hygiene*, Vol. 10, 1967, pp. 255–61.

| Mean age | 54.7 | 53.5 | 53.7 | 55.3 | | 55.0 | 55.2 | 59.8 | 54.8 |
| Mean years of exposure | 18.2 | 21.3 | 21.2 | 21.8 | | 31.5 | 35.5 | 30.5 | 36.4 |

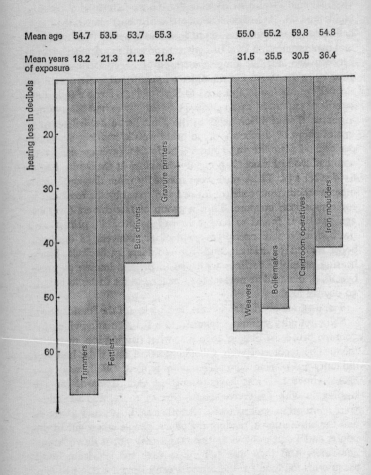

exposure to high noise levels. There is a type of noise-induced deafness, called temporary threshold shift, which is a passing numbing. After the noise has ceased or the shift ended, the hearing returns. But some degrees of sound pressure are too much for the ear, which is a sensitive instrument, especially in children who can hear sounds up to 20,000 cycles per second, like the very high-pitched tone that U.H.F. (625 line) television sets give off. The ear has three parts, outer, middle and inner. The outer and visible ear collects sounds and transmits them down the auditory canal to the eardrum. The middle ear transmits and identifies these sound vibrations; it is an air-filled cavity bridged by three bones – the hammer, anvil and stirrup. The hammer, attached to the eardrum, vibrates with it and works with the anvil as a bent lever to vibrate the stirrup.

Damage to any of these three bones can cause deafness, since vibrations now do not reach the inner part of the ear, the cochlea. This organ is a helical tube filled with liquid and lined with hair-like projections of different lengths. Continuous high noise levels damage these hair-like objects, and since the role of the cochlea is to transform vibrations into nerve impulses, which are sent along the auditory nerve to the brain and there interpreted as sounds, the result is critical. The signals along the auditory nerve get indistinct.

What is it like to be a victim of noise-induced hearing loss? Rupert Taylor, a young noise consultant who advises industries about their noise problems, has described what an audiometrician would find when he tests the hearing of someone who has been working in a very high noise level of around 110 dBA for a few days:

... the audiometrician would put headphones on you in a quiet room, and a machine would play quiet tones through the headphones while you signalled that you could or could not hear anything. Starting at the bottom of the frequency scale and going up in octaves, your hearing sensitivity would be good, until you got to 2,000 Hz (about three octaves above middle 'C') where you would not be so good. An octave higher, and the machine would have to be turned up by about 20 decibels for you to hear it.

You could be taken off work at this stage, or even after a considerably longer period of time, given a quiet job and after a few weeks or even months your hearing would come back to within tolerable limits. But if you stay in the noisy job there comes a point of no return, and the damage starts to become permanent and irreversible. After 20 years the hearing test will show a 40–50 decibel drop in sensitivity around this critical frequency band between 2,000 and 8,000 Hz. After another ten or fifteen years, frequencies on either side will be dragged down too so that your hearing will be very bad at any frequency above 500 Hz, and there is nothing you could do about it.[3]

With this in mind, consider the results of a questionnaire on noise that the Industrial Welfare Society sent out to member firms in 1962. The society was trying to discover how many workers in each company worked in conditions so noisy that he was unable to speak to his fellow workers – he was isolated by noise. A textile firm had 75 per cent of its 2,264 workers isolated; a ship-repairing company had 90 per cent of its 1,464 workers in that condition. All of the 1,080 workers in a heavy engineering company qualified and so did 90 per cent of 1,115 workers in a factory producing jam jars and bottles. Perhaps appropriately, 53 per cent of the 310 workers in a coffin maker's were in the same condition. A number of other firms, ranging from rayon-yarn manufacturers to drop forgers to printers, had over half their workers isolated by noise. And the total from all the fifty-five firms that answered the questionnaire indicated that 24 per cent of the workers were so isolated.

I would guess that this is probably close to the actual figure for all of British industry. (One is reduced to guessing, since a complete survey of the extent of industrial deafness has never been done.) I say this because even the industries – like agriculture – which once did not expose their workers to loud noise – now do so. The tractor driver today, ploughing his furrow in a rural peace with rooks or seagulls following behind as they have always done, may be working in appallingly noisy conditions. Most modern tractors have cabs which entrap the noise. Their drivers in fact are in great danger of going deaf, a fact which one tractor manufacturer has recognized by providing a free set of ear muffs

3. *Daily Telegraph Magazine*, 11 June 1971.

with each tractor sold. (Much cheaper to provide muffs than to quieten the tractor.)

The condition – 'isolated by noise' – is useful because it is almost certain that any worker so affected is at least at risk of having his hearing damaged, perhaps very gravely. Rupert Taylor considers this to be true, and himself estimates that people at risk from noise at work run into 'many thousands'. He reckons, in his Pelican study *Noise*, that employees of about 5,000 companies are in danger of becoming deaf. Interestingly, he records that an acoustic engineer told him that amplifiers of cinemas in industrial areas of the North are usually on a higher setting than those in suburban parts of the South.

These then are vast numbers of people affected; finally the total may be found to be yet larger; it is being recognized that the lorry cab is one of the noisiest workplaces in the country; so are bus cabs. The numbers of lorry drivers and bus drivers are legion.

In 1971 hearing damage among coal miners was featured in a study completed by the National Coal Board. It is the results of a check on the hearing of miners in the Yorkshire Coal Field. The Coal Board first tried to test men who had worked for long periods on one type of machine – men who were 'machine pure' in the jargon. The Coal Board's doctors hoped they could then match a decline in hearing ability to the level of noise the miner was exposed to – a level that would be known by testing the type of machine.

In the event 'the machine pure' were elusive; too many miners had shifted their jobs around in the pit. The Coal Board settled for a different strategy. It tested miners who had been injured at work and were recovering in one of the Board's rehabilitation centres. The Board then went back into the men's histories and eliminated those who had served in the armed forces, had defective hearing through disease, and so on. In the end 394 miners were tested. The results showed that about half of the men had appreciable hearing loss attributable to industrial noise. As one would expect, the men were mainly older miners, and of course the sample could not be said to be statistically representative of all Britain's miners.

None the less the results are worrying, even if the Coal Board strategically claims that it is not possible to say that the degree of damage the miners have suffered ranks as an industrial injury. But the results are not incredible. Miners often work in very high noise levels in enclosed spaces. The National Coal Board has machines, particularly the pneumatic tools like the air-leg borer, a tunnel drill, which produces noise levels over 100 decibels, which is well into the danger area for human hearing. And although the air-leg borer is only used for short periods at a stretch – to bore the holes for the explosive charges at the coal face – miners have to work for longer periods with machines that produce between 90 and 100 decibels. Some of these miners damage their hearing. So do some men in the coal washeries – a full eight-hour shift exposure to high noise levels. And by 1971 the Coal Board's methods of defence lay not so much in reducing the noise of machines themselves, but in giving the men breaks in quiet canteens, where their buzzing ears could rest awhile. 'Noise breaks' do serve a good purpose in conserving hearing, but they are no substitute (as we shall see) for reducing the noise at source.

Countless cases like this exist in British industry today. Noise often is the norm. Along with many other types of pollution, noise shares the feature of transferring a cost from the people making the noise (or permitting it to occur; or profiting indirectly) to the people suffering the noise. Polluters in this way externalize their pollution-control costs; they pass them on to others. The firm that uses noisy pneumatic drills for its orders passes the cost of silencing (or depolluting) the drill on to (at least) the man who operates it. Indirectly the operator pays in decreased enjoyment and increased social embarrassment. Directly, he may pay for it in ways like having to buy a hearing aid. Aircraft noise pollution is another example. The airlines flying Boeing 707s or V.C.10s buck the cost of operating quieter aircraft (either the earlier generation turbo-props like Viscounts, Vanguards, Britannias or the new generation jets, the by-pass Boeing 747 jumbo aircraft) The people who pay are those living near the airports, paying indirectly in losing sleep, pleasure and probably working efficiency, and directly in having their houses soundproofed and their windows double-glazed. Facts like these led the government's Noise Advisory Council to maintain that it is a person's right to be able to live in reasonable quiet. If in the course of living or working he is subjected to high noise levels, then his right is being infringed.

Industrial noise in some cases may be one of those pollutions in which the polluter also pays. (This is not true, say, of a local authority with an inefficient sewage works; the people down river pay.) There is evidence that some kinds of noise make people work much less well. Philip Beales, the ear, nose and throat surgeon, writes in his book *Noise Deafness and Hearing* (Michael Joseph, 1965): 'In an electronics factory in the Home Counties noisy conditions caused 110 assembly workers to make 60 mistakes in 24 hours, but once the surroundings were changed, reducing the noise, only seven mistakes were made in the same time.'

Some of these tests must be looked at twice. An experiment in the thirties showed that typists improved their speed of work when their rooms were made quieter. But they also improved it when the sound in the room was put back to its original level. Again psychologist Donald Broadbent, now director of the Medical Research Council's Applied Psychology Research Unit at Cambridge, and E. A. J. Little, showed in an experiment in 1960 that Kodak employees working with film-perforating machines worked faster when their room was made quieter by about ten decibels, but also showed the same improvement when they were placed in rooms that had not been quietened. The reason for the improvements was that the workers liked having some attention paid to them.[4]

It has also been shown that sometimes people work better when the noise level is increased. Primarily it seems to operate as a stimulant to tired minds. An American university researcher, Dr William Wokoun showed that people working on a task similar to that of a radar operator reacted well to piped music while they worked. The improvement, however, was particularly marked towards the end of the work period – it kept them from flagging. Dr Donald Broadbent has also shown from studies of naval ratings watching twenty steam-pressure dials and turning a

4. *Occupational Psychology*, Vol. 34, No. 133, 1960.

knob at a critical reading that a high sound level makes little difference when the rating has to watch simply one dial. When, however, he has to switch his attention from one dial to several, his concentration is marred by the higher noise level.[5] This seems the crucial point: noise at higher levels acts as a distraction in tasks where a number of rapid judgements are needed.

Researchers Donald Broadbent and E. A. J. Little in their tests with the photographic workers found that they made far fewer mistakes – breaking the film, or stopping the machines by threading the film incorrectly – in rooms where the sound level had been reduced than where the noise level had been left as it was. In the 'untreated rooms' the men worked in a sound level of ninety-eight decibels – pretty high – and were found to improve their work rate under study – because of the morale factor, because they liked getting some attention. In fact, the men in the un-soundproofed rooms had as good an output as the men in the quietened rooms, but they had five times the number of breakages.

In the thirties some cotton weavers were put through their paces. They were given ear plugs, which reduced the noise by ten to fifteen decibels. But the weavers disliked the plugs, and said they didn't think they would improve their work. Yet in the end they were prevailed upon to wear them and their efficiency rose by about twelve per cent.

By and large, research is proving two things. First it is showing that moderate sound, below eighty-five decibels, makes little difference one way or the other. Secondly, it is showing that noise above this level does affect performance and particularly in complex tasks that require many judgements to be made. In this kind of work the high noise level increases the number of mistakes. To summarize, it has been proved that noise damages human beings and that often it also damages their efficiency. That amounts to a wholesale condemnation of noise in industry.

Yet, curiously, noise remains the Cinderella in industrial pollution. It does not arouse the passions of industrial accidents or handicaps like blindness. If the foundry workers had been discovered by Dr Gordon Atherley and his co-workers to be walking

5. *Quarterly Journal of Experimental Psychology*, Vol. 6, No. 1, 1954.

out of the factory gates tapping with white sticks, a great public clamour would rightly have been set up. The late John Barr made this same point in his book *The Assaults on our Senses* (Methuen, 1970):

> There are about 112,000 blind people in the nation, about two million deaf, yet the National Institute for the Deaf has a capital of only £400,000. The leading blind charities have about ten times as much; St Dunstan's has about £17,000,000 to aid only 2,000 war blinded. Wireless for the Blind appeals draw immense support; a recent television for the Deaf appeal brought in only £20,000.

I believe these attitudes and priorities reflect simply the much greater fear that people have at losing their sight than their hearing. It needs only a little imagination, however, to understand how isolating deafness is. The deaf or part-deaf person finds it much harder to communicate with people than the blind. The telephone, the radio or the television are no comfort to him. Often it is harder for the person severely handicapped by deafness to get a job; employers don't take to people who can't use the telephone, can't communicate with their fellow workers. The deaf are also figures of fun, where the blind are objects of sympathy. The special nastiness of Vladimir Nabokov's *Laughter in the Dark* was partly in his flouting of the usual codes of behaviour towards the blind; the reader suffers for the blind man cuckolded in the very room he lives in.

For the problem of industrial deafness, these attitudes are compounded by shopfloor attitudes from both management and men. I have visited foundries in Birmingham where men were exposed to the explosive noise of drop forges, and the men have smiled to see me wince and cover my ears. I have talked to factory workers living eight hours or more a day in sound levels around 100 dBA and been told 'The noise is part of the job; it's what you expect in an industry like this.' Work and noise is a pairing that they and their fathers before them have been brought up to accept.

Managements have been content to share and exploit these feelings. At a Birmingham drop forge, a company manager answered me frankly when I asked how many of their workers are deafened: 'We never get complaints. I don't think we have deafened any because most of our workers come from other foundries and they're already deaf by the time we get them.' At another foundry in the same city, the works manager shouted to me above the noise 'Why don't these men have ear defenders? We give them cotton wool, and they won't wear anything else.' Cotton wool is quite useless at protecting hearing from high noise levels. Both these conversations took place in 1971.

This kind of brute, complacent, paunch reaction to industrial noise must make way for a rational, scientific and humane approach. We must have quiet processes, quiet machines, quiet shopfloors and protected workers.

The essential ground clearing for this has already been done: the work of two men, William Burns, Professor of Physiology in the University of London at Charing Cross Hospital School and Dr D. W. Robinson, head of the Acoustics section of the National Physical Laboratory. Commissioned by the government into examining hearing and noise in industry, the final Burns–Robinson report that appeared in 1970 made a number of important advances. None was more useful than their clear demonstration that hearing is impaired as a result of the combined effect of the intensity of the noise to which the worker is exposed and the duration of that exposure. Burns and Robinson devised a formula from which we can predict the ranges of hearing losses we can expect from continuous exposure to sound of different levels.

This formula, a combination of duration and intensity, is crucial. Applied properly, it should enable workers to be protected. Burns and Robinson emphasize that the level of noise which we in the end judge as permissible must depend on the amount of risk we are prepared to take. The higher the noise level, the greater the chance that some workers, a minority only perhaps, will suffer permanent hearing damage. Burns and Robinson themselves suggest a maximum level of ninety decibels on the A scale most commonly used, for an eight-hour daily exposure. Any increase in sound level above this point, say Burns and Robinson, must be accompanied by a fifty per cent reduction in exposure. A doubling in noise level – from 90 dBA to 100, remembering that the decibel scale is logarithmic and each increase of ten decibels on the A scale represents a doubling – should be accompanied by a reduction of the exposure by four hours. Finally Burns and Robinson make an absolute overriding condition that no unprotected ear should ever be exposed to a sound pressure level of 135 decibels or more.

The two researchers have been much castigated for their ninety decibel for eight hours formula, particularly as it is passing into law. The Noise Abatement Society in particular has regarded it as nicely convenient for industry. The society advocates, and I believe it is right, a much lower level, of eighty-five decibels. But, even if Burns and Robinson erred here, their real contribution was the advocating of the formula principle: intensity plus duration.

Some companies have already been operating on this principle. Esso Petroleum have zoned their refinery at Fawley, Hampshire, selecting especially noisy areas. Before a worker enters such a zone he passes a notice which tells him that his stay in that area must be limited to ten minutes or one hour – according to the noise level present – unless the worker is wearing ear defenders. This is the type of action that should be taken wherever there is a machine that cannot be itself silenced.

Stone Manganese Marine, one of the two foundries studied by the Manchester University researchers, also employ such methods, providing ear defenders and giving the trimmers and fettlers twenty minutes off work in every hour. It is not clear how successful such methods have been at Stone Manganese. For Frank Berry, who worked at their Charlton shop, the company's protection methods were inadequate. In 1967, when Berry joined the company, it stocked two sizes of ear plugs out of five or possibly seven. Berry was given a choice of size. But expert witnesses at the case of *Berry* v. *Stone Manganese Marine* told the judge that the selection of the right ear plugs could not be left to an untrained layman – some form of supervision was required. In December 1971 Mr Justice Ashworth found that the company were in breach of their duty to take reasonable care in the matter of the ear plugs. He also found the company in breach of their duty to Frank Berry by not supplying ear muffs.

'Ear defenders' – ear muffs to the man in the street – alone are absolutely no long-term solution. Industrialists often favour tackling complaints about high noise levels by providing ear defenders, mainly because it is cheap. As noise consultant Rupert Taylor told me, 'It's absolutely no solution for the works manager just to leave a pile of muffs in the corridor and let the worker get on with it.'

It is no solution for several reasons. For one thing, ear defenders are not much more popular with workers than are ear plugs, which many workers say are uncomfortable. Workers complain that the muffs are bulky. ('After my members have put on their muffs and their steel helmets, they look like Santa Claus,' one union leader said to me.) They complain that they make it hard to communicate with their workmates and hard to listen to 'useful sounds' like warning noises.

Many of these complaints are quite unjustified. Many types of ear defenders don't cut out speech and there are some on the market that incorporate an electronic device which transmits quiet sound (i.e. speech) but cuts out loud sound. However, it must be faced that many workers – miners especially – *won't* wear ear muffs. We must thus act accordingly, just as we require motor-car manufacturers to produce safer products, for people who have safety belts fitted by law in their cars but won't wear them. For another thing, ear defenders are not good at protecting the ear from low-frequency sound, which can be very damaging.

However, workers who have suffered damaged hearing should take note of Frank Berry's case against his employers, Stone Manganese Marine. Berry's hearing was being damaged for several years before he actually consulted his trade union in 1968. But once he had given them the case, the trade union took it up. Unions do not have a great record on industrial noise; they have tended to concentrate on hours and pay, and reflect the view that noise and industry are just inseparable bedfellows. We must therefore hope that trade unions are now taking a broader view of their responsibilities and that workers who suspect their hearing is damaged by rackety machines and inadequate protection will seek their advice.

Progress can be made in re-designing the lay-out of factories. If a noise level is deafening, it may be because too many moderately noisy machines are in one shed. Separate or screen them off, and the problem will be cut. Compressors are a good example of machines that should be segregated from the main work areas. Walls should be built thicker and heavier than they are now, in preference to the light, cheap stuff beloved by the cost accountants. Sound-absorbent building material can be used – and so on. But again, these improvements skirt round the heart of the matter: the machine itself, the source of the noise. It's here that attention should centre. And the basic principle should be to design quietly in the first place. It is much more effective to try to reduce the noise from the machine when it is on the drawing board than when it's on the factory floor. But many design engineers still do not think of acoustic aspects until after the prototype stage. Rupert Taylor puts it: 'The designer considers what sort of machine he wants, designs it, builds it, starts it up. Then he says "What a racket!" and tries to tinker about to quieten it. Then it's too late.' Taylor adds: 'What we've got to do is to get economic pressure on the designer to design quietly.'

Already consumers are making their feelings about noise felt. Manufacturers like Perkins Diesel find that more and more often they are asked to supply acoustical details about a machine. 'What's the dBA?' is a question that's going to be asked almost as often as 'What's the price?' British design engineers, sadly, are not always well equipped to cope with this new mood. Many degree courses in engineering do not take in acoustics in more than a cursory way. Today universities and technical institutes are at last starting to gear themselves to an acoustical age. The Open University, in its first year, has included acoustics in some courses. At the early design stage such expertise will be needed. Great improvements can be secured: the Factory Inspectorate points to the marked noise reduction with parts moving at high speeds if aerodynamic techniques are applied. Design changes such as using solid polyurethene or nylon parts in place of metal can cut noise.

Engines also can be quietened. C.A.V. Ltd, who make fuel injectors for diesel engines, were irritated by criticisms that the diesel noise was due to the injector. To prove their case, they built a quiet diesel engine. Or rather they built two quiet diesel engines, one with highly damped walls, the other with different materials for the cylinder block and crankcase. The second type of engine in particular was very successful – reducing the noise to that of petrol engines, and eliminating the notorious knock of the diesel engine. But for this exercise C.A.V. incurred the displeasure of the motor-car industry, after the C.A.V. engine was featured on the B.B.C. television programme Tomorrow's World. The industry did not take kindly to proof that it can build quieter engines than it does.

Design improvements like these must really be worked at. Too often it is true that the new machines being installed in factories are no better or even worse than their venerable predecessors. Often the trouble is that the new machines, though intrinsically of better design, are run at higher speeds and are thus noisier. Some Belgian Picanol looms installed in some of the jute mills in Dundee are noisier than the very old machines they replaced because they are very much faster.

The speed problem also bedevils attempts to reduce noise in the Lancashire cotton mills. In 1969 the Factory Inspectorate checked the noise levels of new and old machines in the mills, and found that installation of the new machines alone would not get noise levels down to a point where the weavers' hearing would be safe. Speeds of new looms were found to be rising, and anyway the slightly quieter shuttleless machines are only a small proportion of the total number of looms. Automatic looms with shuttles are still being installed and will be in use for many years. These looms were found to be yet noisier than the older non-automatic looms which run at slower speeds.

To complete an unhappy picture, the Factory Inspectorate found the really useful design changes were 'usually considered uneconomic for production machines and in practice it is unusual for textile machines to incorporate measures solely intended to reduce the sound level'. All the looms measured produced sound levels above eighty-five dBA, and only one type was in any way producing 'safe sound' – i.e. below ninety dBA.

The people most damaged by industrial noise are obviously those right in the thick of it: the operators of the machines, the factory workers. But industrial noise injures also a much larger audience. It is a pollution cost passed on to people outside the factory gates, indeed sometimes a mile or more from the gates. Complaints from people living within sound of industrial processes are rising rapidly. Many people are having their sleep disturbed and their lives marred by background sounds provided gratis by a drop hammer or a compressor.

A typical example was a London metal-recovery firm, which worked one plant in London six days a week, day and night. The plant lived on a diet of old tin cans and waste-metal strip from boxes and cans; it recovered the metal. People living near the factory were treated to a kind of industrial concert. There were rattles as avalanches of tin cans were tipped by lorries; rattles and grinds as a mechanical shovel lifted the cans on to a conveyor belt; rattles, grinds and thumps as a metal shaker was used to separate paper and rubbish from the cans. Contributions came also from bales of tin cans being thrown on to a metal conveyor belt, the heavy percussion of a hammer mill used to break up the bales, and shrieks from two overhead cranes. Through day and night the concert went on.

Problems like these are becoming more widespread. In 1969 the Labour Government received reports from local authorities in England and Wales about their industrial noise problem – that is, the industrial noise the public hears. Sixty per cent of local authorities replied (876). Of these 385 said they had a 'serious' noise problem, and that group included all but six of the 96 London and County Boroughs reporting. Some 350 said they had no industrial noise problem, but many of these were rural district councils or urban councils with little heavy industry in their areas. A group of 141 local authorities said they had a 'slight' problem.

In addition, the complaints about noise nuisance are increasing steadily. Local authorities get about ten per cent more complaints each year, says the Association of Public Health Inspectors. It is said that about half all the complaints are found to be justified by investigation – this is a very high proportion. The association made contact with 705 local authorities on the question and found that in 1969 a total of 2,355 cases of industrial-noise nuisance had been identified. This may be the tip of an iceberg. All in all, the evidence is that the industrial noise problem is getting worse.

The growing public anger is due to several factors. The most important is that modern industrial processes are often noisier than the equipment they replaced. The traditional 'backyard' industry also has re-equipped itself; the process going on at the bottom of someone's garden may once have been a manual one; now it may be powered by a diesel engine, thumping away all day. Again, fewer people today live by the factories they work in – a fact which makes them much more inclined to protest at the factories' pollution. The blockade of the factory in Swansea, United Carbon Black's works at Port Tennant, in February 1971 bears out this point though in reverse. The works was blockaded by local residents, mainly housewives, complaining about air pollution. Interestingly, only a few of the factory's seventy-odd workers lived near by; the actual local residents had little for which to be beholden to United Carbon Black.

The evidence is also that the public is most abused by pneumatic drills, with air compressors and fans following close behind. Handling of materials (especially metal) and lorry deliveries (especially the clang of beer kegs on pavements) are also prominent.

In the ineffable British way, most of these complaints are handled in an informal way, with the local public-health inspector grumbling at the local employer. Indeed, over ninety per cent of confirmed industrial noise nuisances are dealt with without any resort to a formal serving of a noise-abatement notice or without recourse to the courts. In any one year only a few hundred abatement notices are served and less than fifty nuisance orders are made by the courts.

Sometimes this informal system works very well. The case of a gas-cylinder firm bears this out. The company built a new factory near residential property and assured residents that there would not be a noise problem. In fact, the loading bay of the plant handled and refilled hundreds of steel cylinders daily; lorries brought empty cylinders back to the factory up until eleven o'clock at night. The trouble was the method of unloading the cylinders: it was crude, and metal cylinder clanged against metal cylinder, making a noise that could be heard up to half a mile away. The people living near by had their rest disturbed and their sleep shattered by these noises off.

The local chief public-health inspector demanded action from the company. His officials and the company's chewed over many solutions, such as fitting rubber rings around the cylinders to prevent the metallic contact; using pallets; or not unloading the cylinders at all but refilling them on the lorry.

The company resisted many of these suggestions, saying that a new method of handling the cylinders would have to be adopted for all its plants in the country, etc., and that the existing method of handling could not be altered for technical reasons, etc., etc. But the chief public-health inspector persevered, insisted. Finally the factory's engineering staff were told to design a system to overcome the problem. They were spectacularly successful. They designed a truck body which allowed the cylinders to be stacked vertically along the sides and down the centre of the body. The cylinders could thus be refilled *in situ*, without any need to unload. But the unloading problem – for that operation had to take place at times – was also overcome. The engineers designed a compressed-air hoist to raise and lower them to or from the vehicle. The system of stacking the cylinders on the loading bay was also completely revised to allow them to be stacked vertically.

The effects of these changes were many. Most important, the new system was quiet. But also, as the system was extended to other depots, the company found additional benefits. Only one man was needed to manage each lorry, as opposed to two previously. The stock at each depot of spare cylinders, it was found, did not need to be so large. The space taken by the cylinders stacked on end was much less than when they were laid flat. As a result existing depots which were overcrowded and needed extending were now adequate. The company saved a considerable amount of money. New depots being planned were built smaller; the wage bill was cut; old depots were given a new lease of life. Again most important, all over the country the sound of cylinder clanging on cylinder was stilled.

In yet another case in which the informal system worked, residents were being startled out of their wits by explosions coming from a scrap-breaking yard about a quarter of a mile from their homes. The firm was investigated by the local authority, who found it using time-dishonoured methods of scrap breaking –

such as using a falling heavy weight for smashing breakable metals, and multiple explosive charges for bursting the larger steel and iron castings. The falling-weight operation was carried out in the open yard on most days of the working week; the explosions occurred at widely separated intervals two or three days a week. It is hard to think of a formula for greater nuisance.

The local authority got the company to make a number of changes. At the end of the cutting nearest to the housing estate where the local people lived, earthworks were raised to act as baffles and to prevent funnelling of the noise. A pit in which the explosives were used was strengthened with armour plating on the sides, a heavier cover was fitted and the sides were raised above ground level to try to deaden the noise. A large number of small explosive charges are now being used instead of the more powerful ones.

Those changes, cumulatively, have cut down the nuisance to a marked degree, in that factory area. But, though it is capable of occasional victories, the existing law, primarily incorporated in the Noise Abatement Act 1960, is quite deficient as an adequate instrument for controlling industrial noise as it affects people outside factory walls, the residents of industrial areas. What is needed is a totally different concept of noise control.

The 1960 Noise Abatement Act has as its lynch-pin the concept of 'nuisance'. I dislike the very term: it smacks of minor irritation when there is much evidence to make us suspect that noise causes suffering and misery. Nuisance has been defined by case law (such as Walter v. Selfe (1851), Vanderpant v. Mayfair Hotel (1930) and Halsey v. Esso Petroleum (1961) as 'an inconvenience materially interfering with the ordinary physical comfort of human existence not merely according to elegant or dainty modes and habits of living but according to plain and sober and simple notions obtaining among English people'. When a local authority, which is required to inspect its district from time to time, believes that a noise nuisance is occurring, it can serve an 'abatement notice' upon the people or industry causing the offence, requiring steps to be taken to reduce the noise. If nothing happens, the local authority must then bring 'complaint' proceedings to a magistrates' court and require the enforcing of the abatement order. If the magistrates are satisfied that a nuisance exists, they must make a 'nuisance order' and they can fine the industrialist concerned for not complying with the original abatement order and require him to undertake any works to keep the noise down.

This procedure, put simply, is the principal manner in which local authorities can combat industrial noise as it affects the public. They are ill-armed. They have no powers to prevent noise occurring; they can only try to abate it after the event; they can really only attack specific nuisances, attributable to a single noise source; they have no power to deal with a multiplicity of sources which cumulatively may be making life most unpleasant for people. Further, they find it very hard to *prove* nuisance. Advocates of 'keep-it-out-of-the-courts' methods make much of the fact that over ninety per cent of confirmed noise nuisances are being dealt with without any use of abatement orders or stern warnings from the magistrates' bench. I believe it is true that in many cases the local authority *must* negotiate informally with an industrialist; he knows it is too hard to get evidence that will stand up in court as the law is fixed now.

An attempt to tackle this problem was made in 1967 when a guide to how to judge a nuisance was laid down with British Standard 4142. This establishes methods of measuring noise levels and for applying the measurements so that the public-health inspector can assess his chances of success in a prosecution. But the trouble is that the British Standard 4142 requires a noise to be markedly louder than the background noise if it is to be rated as a nuisance. It thus totally fails to deal with the common urban problem of noise levels generally rising – a higher 'ambient' noise level. As the ambient creeps up, perhaps because of more noise sources, so the industrialist may make more noise without the public-health inspector being equipped to fight him.

These criticisms of the Noise Abatement Act 1960 were made very recently in *Neighbourhood Noise*, the report of a working group of the government's Noise Advisory Council that was set up to see how the Act was working. I was one of the six members of the group which was chaired by Sir Hilary Scott, a past president of the Law Society. *Neighbourhood Noise* is being considered by the government and may be the subject of debate in Whitehall and Westminster. The civil servants and the members of Parliament may spend most time upon one suggestion our working group made. To my mind it is the most radical advance we made, a crucial change. It is the recommendation that 'Noise Abatement Zones' be created by local authorities, we expect especially in those urban areas where people live in the shadow of factories. It is a proposal that may be strongly opposed by some industrialists, who may argue especially that it is unworkable. The industrialists, certainly as represented by the Confederation of British Industry, which gave evidence to the working group, would prefer a small group of experts similar in function to the Alkali Inspectorate, who would advise and control industries with especially intractable noise problems.

We opted for our much broader approach, believing that industry is policed by sufficient groups of peripatetic experts (such as the Factory Inspectorate and the Alkali Inspectorate) as it is. What we want to do is to reduce the 'ambient level' in these areas, the background clangour. The local authorities would have the power to create Noise Abatement Zones in any part of their district where they believed there is a bad neighbourhood noise problem. The authorities' public-health inspectors would make an inspection of the district and fix target emission levels in dBA that a firm would have to comply with. The target level would most usually be measured at the perimeter of the factory, and the factory owners would have at least six months in which to make the necessary alterations, whether silencing machinery or building new curtain walling, to comply with the target level. In any Noise Abatement Zone you would expect to find a variety of firms with a variety of target levels. Any new industrialist moving into the zone would be required, on being given planning permission, to comply with his target emission level right from the start. In this way we felt that a real attack could be mounted both on the noisiest factories and on the steady creep-creep of the ambient level.

The industrialist would be adequately protected from persecution-minded public-health inspectors. If he was prosecuted for not having attained his target emission level, it would be a defence to show that he was meeting his general duty to use the 'best practicable means' to reduce his noise. This phrase exists, much qualified, in the 1960 Act and is rarely (perhaps too rarely) rigidly interpreted. He could also fight the whole designation of the area in which his plant was situated and his target level by objecting to the Secretary of State for the Environment.

Some industrialists, however, will fight the zones idea tooth and claw. It gives more power to the public-health inspector, who industry knows is answerable to the public, and less amenable than a central agency directed from a Whitehall office. These industrialists may argue especially that it is technically unsound, that it is not possible to measure the noise of Factory A because it is too close to Factory B (forgetting that it is rare for both A and B to be *always* operating simultaneously), that industries will be priced out of markets by the new anti-noise-pollution standards. Most of these objections are comprehensively considered in the *Neighbourhood Noise* report itself. But it is worth making two further points. One is to counter the 'poverty' plea, the charge that industrialists could be put out of business. Past experience gives this little credence. The American automobile industry pleaded bankruptcy when the United States government, spurred by Ralph Nader's disclosures, demanded tough safety standards in automobiles. In the event the standards were met, the costs were much lower than had been predicted, and absolutely no one went bankrupt. But in the unlikely event of such a plea being soundly based, we can remember that Peter Walker said at the start of his office as Secretary of State for the Environment that 'the polluter shall pay' for the pollution he causes. Put differently, this means that the polluting firm shall no longer pass on these costs to other people – perhaps neighbouring dwellings shaken by industrial noise.

The other point is to stress the value of Noise Abatement Zones as a spur also to local authorities. They will enable the public to remonstrate with a comatose authority in a district with severe noise problems. 'How many zones have you created?' the authority can be asked. Just as indolent authorities with bad smoke problems have rightly been castigated for failing to create the smoke-control areas, so also will local authorities be open to the same charges on noise.

The war on noise, if it is to be waged effectively, will need engineering improvements to match the legal changes. Like the noise in the factory that deafens the worker, so the noise that drives the housewife neurotic can at the last count only really be tackled at source. The primary source of trouble is the noisy machinery itself. Quietness must be built in at the design stage. The construction industry, often the residents' greatest bugbear, has examples to show what can be done. Thus, when the Hyde Park Underpass was under construction, some interesting special methods were adopted because of the proximity of St George's Hospital. A way was found to rivet the sides of the excavation without the use of driven sheet piling. And the Hendon Urban Motorway gave some improvements, again because people were living very near to the building operations. Piles were driven by hydraulic pressure instead of the normal thunderous drop hammer; timber planking was used between occasional king piles instead of the reverberating sheet-metal piling.

Some of the equipment used in road works can be silenced. Compressors today are much quieter than earlier models, partly because of excellent work done by the Institute of Sound and Vibration Research at the University of Southampton. Muffles on pneumatic drills can drop noise levels by 10 dBA, while a French company has introduced a hydraulically driven road drill which has a noise level under 75 dBA when two drills and one compressor are operating.

Other improvements can be made by altering the buildings in which processes are taking place, or indeed putting the process inside a building where it was not before. The light factory walls attractive for their cheapness are here as much a problem to the people outside the factory as they are to the workers within. The Association of Public Health Inspectors has urged, rightly, that the best way to ensure noise is kept to a minimum is by designing the building or modifying it for the machinery it is to contain *before* the machine is installed and running. Dealing with a noise nuisance after it has been created is nearly always unsatisfactory. We must prevent, not patch and mend.

Chapter 5

The World's Largest Brick Maker

People pay today the price of a society that permitted industrialists to produce and pollute without restraint. The working classes of Lancashire, to take an example, have inherited rivers like the Irwell or the Gowy that are often little more than a cheap means of conveying waste from factories. But the worst of their inheritances from those changes that occurred almost 150 years ago, collectively called the Industrial Revolution, is bad lands. The county is pitted by thousands of disused pit shafts; the sites of many are unknown. (The National Coal Board estimates vaguely that there are about 8,000 shafts.) It has a gargantuan slice of land officially regarded as derelict – more than any other county: sixteen per cent of the total derelict land in England in 1969. The worst of it is that the derelict land is concentrated in old industrial areas. In 1970 more than a quarter of the land east of Wigan was derelict, the result of closed collieries and redundant workings. There for many years the most prominent hills on the landscape were three massive pit heaps, known locally as the Wigan Alps, or the Three Sisters.

Dereliction has the worst social consequences in areas of declining industries. In Lancashire pit and mill closures have been commonplace – more than a thousand textile mills closed in the North-West between 1951 and 1969. The people in these depressed areas face at once a shattered past and bleak future, in a landscape of slag heaps that burn quiet internal fires, turning the air acrid with sulphur, and in an atmosphere of social-security relief and redundancy.

The task of restoring the derelict districts is simply vast. Lancashire County Council started restoring land in 1956, and up to the end of 1969 it reclaimed 700 acres. Yet, as collieries closed, the council found it was not even keeping up with the problem: in 1969 alone more than 1,000 additional acres fell into the official classification of derelict and became the county council's responsibility.[1]

1. Lancashire figures are taken from 'The Reclamation of Lancashire', a

Polluting Britain: A Report

The government's idea of dereliction is an absurd administrative convenience, at odds with the physical facts. Land is only termed derelict and thus open to grant aid from central government for restoration if it is 'land so damaged by industrial or other development that it is incapable of beneficial use without treatment'. This definition excludes land that has become 'naturally' derelict. It ignores agricultural land that has been neglected, or land ravaged by the armed forces. Worst of all, it excludes land that is part of an active industrial site. The smouldering slag heaps of a still working colliery do not qualify. For county councils like Lancashire, the definition is a gross hindrance, since it causes the county to be suddenly granted several hundred acres of derelict land, with the official imprimatur, when a colliery closes.

The Conservative administration that took office in June 1970 has done nothing to alter this interpretation. It has, however, shown itself sensitive to the physical problems of land reclamation and has encouraged larger reclamation programmes. Lancashire County Council's reclamation budget increased sixfold from the financial year 1969–70 to a £300,000 figure for 1970–71. Three quarters of this sum is paid from central government funds. Secretary of State for the Environment, Peter Walker, visited six of the counties with the worst derelict land problems a year after taking office in 1970. He pledged himself to clearing the derelict land (Whitehall interpretation) in the counties that get central government aid by the end of the seventies.

At one time even this limited target seemed beyond the authorities. If it is attained, however, only one aspect of the basic shovel-and-rake task will have been done. Some soured lands will have been re-contoured, cleaned up, re-seeded and drained. Central government reclamation funds, however, are not provided for all the rejuvenation that must be done to prevent the land starting again the slide back to dereliction. For where you find derelict land, you find decaying, rotting housing. Where you find waste-spoil heaps, you find bad schools and deprived children.

---

paper read to the Manchester Statistical Society on 9 December 1970 by D. Tattersall, assistant county planning officer.

Where you find old industrial workings, you find bad roads, poor social services, poor employment, poor people. A huge and massive attack on total social dereliction is necessary to a lasting success: the derelict land is really only the most visible symptom. New communities on the old soured lands may be built in some places, but the odds remain against this becoming the general pattern. Local authorities with the worst dereliction problems reflect their populations; they are not wealthy. Much of the cost of building in houses, schools, roads, health clinics, libraries, parks, civic centres, swimming pools, shopping centres must be paid from a local authority fund ill-fed by rates.

But Conservative promises to clear derelict land in the worst areas within the decade will also be deceptive because the land excluded by the Department of the Environment interpretation will still exist, gathering local bedsteads and trash, yielding crops of ragged robin, thistle and bindweed. Worse, new land will be made derelict by industrial workings, and again will be outside the official definition. The total amount of derelict land in Britain is *growing*, not shrinking, despite the reclamation programmes. Even the government's figures reflect this trend: they show that between 1964 and 1969 in England and Wales, 15,000 more acres were added to make a final derelict total of 114,700 acres. John Barr pointed out this acreage is 'larger than the whole of Rutland, or the combined municipal areas of Manchester, Cardiff and Birmingham'.[2] But if you take a layman's definition of 'derelict', the figures swell further. The Civic Trust has estimated that the net addition to derelict land is about 3,500 acres annually. Mineral workings have been calculated by Professor Gerald Wibberley to be adding land at a gross rate of 12,000 acres to the total. John Barr in 1969 estimated that the total true acreage of derelict land was about a quarter of a million acres – a figure he compared to the area of Huntingdonshire. Such a large swath of Britain emphasizes the need for treating land as a precious resource. Mineral workings make derelict so much first-class farmland in a manner that does not percolate into government statistics until the mining has ceased, excavated, worked out. They must be regulated to minimize their despoliation. Mining

2. *Derelict Britain*, Penguin Books, 1969.

companies must use as little land as necessary; they must restore
as much as possible. What has happened in the counties of Huntingdonshire and Bedfordshire proves the case.

A study of one company, London Brick, the biggest brick
makers in the world, shows that we need a new planning approach to industrial excavations.

The Bedfordshire brickfield has been described in this way:

> In land use terms, the area is still basically rural in character but
> the activities associated with brickmaking dominate the landscape; the
> batteries of tall chimneys, the gaping holes of active and derelict clay
> workings, the constant flow of brick-laden lorries, the sight and smell
> of effluent from the chimneys; all in all a depressing experience.

This passage was written by Geoffrey Cowley, Bedfordshire's
county planner, in *Bedfordshire Brickfield*, the study published in
1967. A year later Cowley made another attempt to describe his
brickfield. This time he drew upon the writings of a man born in
1628 at the village of Elstow, which is now in the heart of the
brickfield: John Bunyan.

> ... they drew near to a very miry Slough, that was in the midst of the
> plain; and they being heedless did both suddenly fall into the bog. The
> name of the Slough was Despond. Here they wallowed for a time,
> being grievously bedaubed with dirt; and Christian, because of the
> Burden that was on his back, began to sink in the Mire.

Christian was rescued by a man called Help. Cowley was sure,
somehow, a contemporary parable could be written, with the
brickfield making a very nice stand-in for the Slough of
Despond.[3]

The brickfield is situated in central Bedfordshire in a valley
that is known locally as Marston Valley, sentimentally as the
Vale of Bedford, and most realistically as 'the Brickworks
Valley'. It is the Bedfordshire excavation of that Oxford clay
formation that runs diagonally across England, from East Yorkshire in the north down in a broad band to Dorset in the south.
From this clay more than 150,000 families a year have their
houses constructed. It provides the bricks for about a third of
all the house building in Britain. This massive brick industry has

3. Brickfield Conference, 1968.

its origins in 1881, when a brick maker at the village of Fletton, near Peterborough, fired his first kiln. The Peterborough field and the Bedfordshire field prosper; so do workings in Buckinghamshire near Calvert and Bletchley. These fields all provide 'flettons' named after that first kiln. London Brick has a near monopoly of the fletton industry having bought out its competitors. In the Peterborough field only a works run by the National Coal Board is competition. In Bedfordshire and Buckinghamshire London Brick is without rivals.

London Brick itself has its origins back in a kiln firing in 1897 at Pillinge, near the brickfield headquarters in the industrial village of Stewartby. This original Forder brickworks grew, absorbed others, was itself absorbed into a much larger company which in 1936, named itself the London Brick Company Ltd. Over the years brick-company takeovers continued. London Brick has always prospered. In 1969 the company took over its chief Bedfordshire rival, the Marston Valley Brick Company. In 1971 London Brick absorbed the last Fletton brickworks owned by Redland, the brick and tile corporation was bought out.

In Bunyan's brickfield London Brick has about 3,000 acres left for clay working. In Peterborough, it has 1,700 acres. From these two fields the company excavates, mainly with drag-line excavators, 150,000 plus tons of clay a week. The company and the two counties, then, have a formidable, continual and growing problem of derelict, redundant land.

How is a profit-motivated enterprise equipped to tackle a pollution problem it necessarily causes, and *knows* it causes?

A visit to Stewartby tells you much about the company. Once it was Wotton Pillinge, a small, poor, insanitary agricultural village. But as the Forder works prospered, brick makers Sir Malcolm and Sir Halley Stewart determined on building a model village, to be named after themselves. Today, in an atmosphere that is a curious mixture of sulphur dioxide and benign paternalism, the families of the men who work in the brick kilns live in neat company houses, set out amid lawns and company-built communal dwellings. Some of the village's 1,100 inhabitants are elderly people, living in seventy-eight single-storey bungalows. To this day the company refers to them as 'old servants' of the company. The bungalows were provided for them out of a trust formed by the late Malcolm Stewart. In fact, if Leyland, home of the trucks and buses, in Lancashire is a company town, it is positively a melting-pot compared to Stewartby, the company village. Stewartby includes a community hall, built in colonial style with colonnades and a good view of a working drag-line hauling up clay. Facing the brickworks is a memorial hall that looks like a New England church. An inscription inside reads: 'Thank God for the men of the Pillinge and Elstow Brickworks who were faithful unto death.' Lists of the dead show whole families worked at the kilns: A. Cox, J. Cox, R. Cox; A. C. Goodman, J. Goodman, W. Goodman; A. S. Caves, A. W. Caves, E. J. Caves, H. J. Caves. Stewartby has also a 'United Church', swimming pool, large playing fields, a company club, and two general stores. A good pension scheme has been running since 1936 and a 'profit-sharing bonus scheme' since 1926.

The company's centre is amid many thousands of acres of its own land, most of it scheduled to be dug up. Around it are 76 active chimneys of its own brickworks, and the farmland run by its own farmers or leased to tenants. To a similar extent this is true of the Peterborough workings, where London Brick works like Kings Dyke are cheek by jowl with London Brick works like Saxon. Perhaps the company finds it hard to view itself objectively, or at least to imagine how others see it. County planner Geoffrey Cowley's description of the valley ('all in all a depressing experience') was contested by a former deputy chairman of the company and a current member of the board, Mr J. P. Bristow. At a public conference on the brickfield organized by Cowley in 1968, Bristow said 'We think it is a scene of intense industrial activity in a country which lives by industry; we don't find it depressing.'

Consider, then, how London Brick makes its products and what happens to the land in the process. First it buys up the agricultural land in the area. Some depth beneath the fairly good farming land, is a precious clay that is the brick makers' boon. It's known as 'knotts' in the industry and is by geological accident so good for its purpose that the bricks almost make themselves. For one thing it contains small whorls or 'knotts' of an oily compound that provides two thirds of the fuel needed for firing. For another, it has an almost constant moisture content, around eighteen to twenty per cent, that allows the clay to be ground into grains, which is a perfect medium for pressing bricks. The newly pressed but as yet unfired brick, known as a 'green', does not have to be stacked for drying out like bricks from other clays. The greens go straight into the kilns. These qualities ensure that the fletton bricks are very competitive in price. Indeed the basic London Brick product, known as a 'commons' in the building industry, is one of the cheapest bricks that can be bought. Low price is one reason why the fletton brick is still so much used long after unwise pundits proclaimed it would be made obsolescent by new building materials and blocks.

But the knotts occur well beneath the fields, on average 10 to 20 feet down, in layers on average 45 to 50 feet thick, and occasionally 100 feet thick. A huge overburden of top-soil, sub-soil and other clays has to be shifted. Drag-line excavators must tear up a layer of 'callow', a brown clay in a layer 10 to 20 feet thick, and often also a blue clay, which has neither the oily compounds nor the dryness of knotts. These waste clays are fed on to conveyor belts and shifted round to part of a brick pit that has already been worked out. Or they are fed on to a mobile 'gantry stacker' that drops the waste well clear of the face, into rows of conical mounds. These huge pimples create a desolate moonscape in a worked-out pit. The actual pit-face, with the brick clay bared, is stripped by huge dragline excavators, which feed hoppers which in turn send the clay to the brickworks, via either railway trucks or conveyor belt or a rope way. Some of the pit faces, where the knott layer is deep, may be 100 feet high and the total acreage of a pit may also be around that figure – though often greater, and growing continuously. A worked-out pit, after a passage of time, is by any stretch of imagination a scene of devastation. Steep-sided, fenced off, little will grow on the 'cold, wet, yellow clay except what grows there now – coltsfoot, weeds, teasels, coarse grasses and the odd bush'.[4]

These vast soured lands are what the brick makers are left with,

4. Mr J. P. Bristow, Brickfield Conference, 1968.

after the digging, the firing and the selling. It is a massive land-pollution problem, outdone in terms of scale and desolation perhaps only by the National Coal Board's tips for colliery slag all over the country. The cubic capacity of the existing pits in Bedfordshire is about eighty-five million cubic yards – to fill them we need as much material as would fill St Paul's Cathedral 200 times. Combined with the complex air-pollution problems caused by brick firing that I describe in Chapter 1, it is inescapable that the London Brick company is doing business at a massive cost to the environment – even if 'it is the national interest that the special qualities of Oxford clay should be exploited', as the Prices and Incomes Board claimed in 1967. Indeed the environmental cost is so great that you can speculate whether such a manner of winning clay would be permitted today.

What then is London Brick's attitude towards restoration, to recompense, to repair, to coming clean? The answer, put crudely, is: what's in it for us? London Brick is a classic example of a joint-stock company, motivated to maximize its return for shareholders, that looks at restoration with interest in the money that can be made from that restoration. This priority, in my opinion, suffuses the company's thinking and it suffuses the very language of its spokesmen. My notebooks contain several quotations from leading executives of London Brick to bear this out: 'We've always had in mind that we've had *assets* in our pits' (Jeremy Rowe, deputy chairman, November 1970). 'Restoration schemes in the past have always fallen down because no one was prepared to pay' (Jeremy Rowe, again). 'We regard these pits as one of our assets and as such have always made a charge, a very reasonable one, for their commercial use in any shape or form' (J. P. Bristow, 1968, Brickfield Conference).

But legislators have long been aware of the cost of London Brick. In 1952 the company got planning permission to excavate clay from further areas in the brickfield, but the Minister for Housing and Local Government in a long, detailed and crucial letter, dated 17 July 1952, indicated to London Brick's estate manager exactly what he wanted. 'The Minister considers', said the official letter,

that the main planning problems presented by these large scale exca-

vations concern the appearance of the sites, both during and after
working, and their ultimate use ... The ultimate aim of restoration
must be in general to fill in these pits completely and so provide a
surface at approximately the original ground level, which can be put
to some further use ... In pursuance of this aim, the Minister pro-
poses to require your Company not only to return all the surplus waste
and overburden arising from the working, but also to fill the excavations with whatever further material may be available. He recog-
nizes that the supply of suitable filling material is likely to be
inadequate for a considerable time to come and that in the meantime
the pits must remain incompletely restored.

The letter continued to indicate interim methods that might be
used, such as tree screening, to minimize the visual offence. But
before finishing it also stipulated, in a critical phrase, the economics of the restoration. In civil-servant instant-death prose, the
stipulation goes like this:

All waste arising from the workings or processing of the clay shall
be deposited in the workings in such a manner, and the excavated areas
shall be further restored by such fillings and levelling as may be
agreed with the local planning authority, having regard in this latter
respect to the *availability of suitable filling materials at suitable times
on reasonable terms*, or to any representations that such materials are
not available, or in the event of disagreement as shall be determined by
the Minister.

The italics are mine. In interpreting the words, London Brick
has been eccentric. The terms imply – hindsight tells us with
insufficient clarity – that London Brick must backfill, provided
that suitable material is available, at a suitable time, at a reasonable *cost*. This implication comes through also in an assent to a
planning application of 1946 by the Marston Valley Brick
Company now part of London Brick: 'The Minister ... has
therefore decided to impose a condition that the Company shall
take such steps as may be within their power to fill the excavation
provided that the material is to be had upon reasonable terms.'

To be had upon reasonable terms; availability on reasonable
terms. London Brick has its own interpretations: to be had upon
terms that will ensure a reasonable profit; availability at reasonable mark-up. I cannot see that this was the Minister's intention.
But J. P. Bristow, at the Brickfield Conference in 1968, publicly

defended his company's eccentric interpretation. He told an audience (that included Niall Macdermot, then Minister of State at the Ministry of Housing) that the company's policy of making a charge for any use of the pits 'fulfills the ministerial conditions as to back filling the pits with "suitable filling materials available at reasonable time and reasonable terms". The planning authorities have been aware for the past fifteen years that we do make such charges and have never challenged them.' (Geoffrey Cowley in his booklet *Bedfordshire Brickfield*, 1967, in fact disputes the brick company's interpretation.)

This is the basis on which London Brick has viewed and weighed almost every solution to the problem of these vast, steep-sided, near-sterile pits, with one exception. The odd pit out is referred to later in the chapter.

The full flowering of this attitude came late in 1970 when London Brick created a separate company to exploit the old pits. The *Guardian* city pages reported: 'London Brick, Britain's biggest brick maker, is diversifying into refuse disposal and leisure – two industries that rank highly in the current list of investment fashions.'

Priority will be given to refuse disposal, an activity that now comes under the anti-pollution banner. Directors indicate that the size of the operation will, within a few years, rival that of Purle Brothers, one of the fastest growing companies on the lists.

In the company of management consultants, London Brick has conducted a two year study of possible diversification moves. At one stage it contemplated a major brick operation in Australia, but the moves now planned will be much more beneficial in terms of short-term profit growth – and market rating.

This new company, named London Brick Land Development, with a few offices at Stewartby, is chaired by Sir Ronald Stewart. The plan is to offer local authorities with a rubbish problem a 'package deal'. Land Development is to set up transfer stations near the main conurbations in a fifty-mile radius of the pits. Council rubbish trucks will deliver the refuse to the stations, where it will be compacted into special containers, taken by road or rail to the pit's side and tipped. The tippings will be compacted, compressed and spread in six-foot layers, with soil between each layer. When the pit is full, it will be covered with soil, and returned either to industrial or agricultural use. The restored land would be the property of London Brick. The company will thus enjoy three stages of profit from the land. It profits from digging out the clay, profits again from charging a filling fee to customers, and profits a third time from using the restored land. It is a masterly application of the principles of profit maximization, an example that should be chalked up on the blackboards of business schools all over the country: an asset is an asset is an asset. But one critic at the Brickfield Conference described the principle as 'like a pickpocket selling back the wallet after he has emptied it'.

But London Brick's latest initiative is inadequate both in practice and in thinking. In practice the new company will not even reverse the despoliation of the Bedfordshire countryside by clay digging. 'Clay will be still taken out at a faster rate than rubbish will be put back,' says Ray Wells, the new manager of London Brick Land Development. He considers that 5,000 tons of rubbish, or 20,000 cubic yards compacted, a week will make the enterprise 'a good commercial undertaking'. But the brick kilns at Stewartby alone consume 50,000 cubic yards of clay a week. London Brick as a whole gorges at least 150,000 cubic yards a week. So deterioration will continue; the effect of the new company will be only to see that matters get worse less rapidly than otherwise would have been the case. And in the Bedfordshire brickfield, where more than 1,500 acres have been dug, there are still almost 3,000 acres waiting to be stripped.

But should not any initiative, however inadequate, be welcomed? Uncontrolled tipping by local authorities, says Jeremy Rowe, deputy chairman, would have been no answer. 'To do it on our scale, £3 to £4 million in the first few years will have to be spent. Refuse will have to be tackled on the sort of scale in which we are in bricks.' There's a lot to this: a string of council rubbish wagons tipping at random, without the waste being compacted or layered, would have been futile, both for the rubbish disposal and the pits. But there is an alternative, a better way, which London Brick's economic structure rejected.

The third way is to allow any local authority to use the pits free of charge. London Brick would take on the cost of transporting the rubbish from the local authorities, of compacting and layering it. Often it would be necessary for London Brick to build and finance the operation of transfer stations near the major conurbations. The cost of these would be only a recompense for the destruction of the landscape. The financing should be arranged according to the original planning consent – 'subject to the availability of suitable filling materials at suitable times on reasonable terms'. Very often London Brick would find waste material on reasonable terms, since the rubbish would be provided gratis with London Brick only picking up the transport and treatment bill. But where the cost of transporting rose sharply the local authority with the rubbish problem and London Brick with the pit problem would have to share the bill, in whatever proportion ensured that the cost to London Brick was 'reasonable'. If London Brick's bill was so high that restoration put the company into financial difficulty, then clearly the terms would not be reasonable.

If London Brick had started acting in this way at the time when it was granted its 1952 planning permissions, great progress could have been made. London alone has spent huge sums in disposing of rubbish; the huge incinerator at Edmonton, opened in 1971, cost £10 million to build, and the treatment costs run in at about £2 per ton of rubbish. Many of the Bedfordshire pits might have been filled had they received London's rubbish, plus that of local towns like Luton, which generates 250 tons of rubbish a day. Ratepayers would have been saved considerable sums; London Brick would have been given a vast quantity of material. It would also still have two stages of profit, with many acres of restored land to enjoy. And the pits are ideally situated for mass refuse disposal. A third of the country's population lies within a fifty-mile radius of these pits – these people generate some seven million tons – or twenty-eight million cubic yards – of refuse a year.

This suggestion is anathema to London Brick. J. P. Bristow put it in 1968: 'Any suggestion that the companies should contribute to the cost of refilling can only mean an increase in the price of bricks at a time when profit margins are already being eroded by ever-increasing costs. How could we then compete with all the materials new and old which flood the market?' This *is* a problem. But it can only be reiterated that no company can be allowed to operate and profit from a mode of working that severely damages the environment. In fact, the generous terms of consent given to London Brick specifically *exclude* the company being put out of business. You could argue that the company is over-protected. Strictly speaking, if the cost of restoration priced the bricks out of the market, my own feeling is that this should be allowed to happen unless the government of the day felt it could not allow such a demise because there are special social grounds – the state of the housing programme. Restoration programmes should then be state subsidized. Strictly speaking, if London Brick's products were undercut by a brick that did not have such environmental consequences in its production, that state of affairs should be accepted. Sadly in my view, the original planning consents ensure London Brick's economic survival. The consents say – clean up if you can afford it. They should have declared – operate cleanly or don't operate at all.

Now it will be hard to persuade London Brick that the consents did not declare: clean up if you can make a reasonable percentage. The reason is that since 1963 some of the company's brick pits around Peterborough are being systematically filled in, a programme that suits the three-profits principle to perfection, as we shall see. In a formidable coup London Brick signed up the Central Electric Generating Board to contribute and supply about fifty million tons of fuel ash from generating stations.

The C.E.G.B. realized in the early sixties that, with demand for electricity doubling every ten years and new power stations being built to match this demand, the Board was facing a formidable surplus of 'P.F.A.' – the pulverized fuel ash left after coal has been crushed and burnt at the power stations. The worst surplus would occur on the generating stations on the River Trent – West Burton (2,000 megawatts) Ratcliffe (2,000 megawatts) and Drakelow (1,450 megawatts). The C.E.G.B. estimated that the new uses to which P.F.A. was being put – in building blocks, as aggregate for concrete and so on – would not match the tonnage of dry ash. Unlike a nineteenth-century enterprise, it did not merely stockpile the surplus in the back yards of power stations. Almost forty per cent of the ash it sold to the building and civil engineering industries, but the remaining sixty per cent was earmarked for the land, mainly in reclamation schemes. (Both grazing and crop culture are possible on fields made of P.F.A. plus a surface of top soil and fertilizer.) The Trent power-station surplus was at first destined for reclamation in the Wash; but the final agreements sent the ash to brick pits. More than 1,000 acres of pit – about a third of London Brick's total excavated area – is already committed for fuel ash. This unique, extraordinary scheme has the ash brought in from the power stations by rail on merry-go-round trains, that always make the same route, stopping to unload at a terminal station in the brickfield and returning to the power stations. In 1961 British Rail calculated that at forty to fifty pence a ton, it would be profitable to transport the P.F.A. The C.E.G.B. then spent £3·5 million on facilities, most of it on the rail terminal. In 1966 the first trains came in; workers hitched air-pressure pipes to blow the fuel out of the wagons, then saw the P.F.A. mixed with water to form a thick wet slurry to be pumped direct into the pits. The ash dried out and hardened. The first square yards of land began to be restored, for farms, or factories, or housing estates.

The trains have run on time since 1966, seven days a week, twenty-four hours a day, seven forty-eight-truck 1,000-ton trains a day. The pits are being filled at the rate of about twenty acres a year: most of the pits in an area north of the terminal are now filled and settling. The grey dried-out fuel ash is out of sight. By a lucky accident, close to the brickfield is a source of top soil. A British Sugar Corporation processing plant has a surplus of many tons of earth, the washings of sugar beets. The top soil is stockpiled and in time spread over the ash in a six-inch layer. The ultimate use of the restored land has yet to be worked out by Huntingdonshire county planners and London Brick.

Heavy expense has fallen to the C.E.G.B. in the scene, and the Board regrets having committed itself so deeply. Every year the ash increases in value and finds new applications. It is used now for a vast range of building products, for a base for new roads and motorways, for a concrete mix.

Initially it was planned for thirty million tons of P.F.A. to be dumped in the pits, over a time scale of at least up to the year 2000. But in 1971 the C.E.G.B. wrote:

The Peterborough scheme is a 'long-stop' for the disposal of ash from several of our new big power stations in the Midlands *when no more economic methods of disposal can be made*. [Their italics.] Increasingly we have been able to find nearer and cheaper sites for disposal and consequently the Peterborough project will take rather longer to complete than we envisaged.

Since London Brick is digging apace at Peterborough, the scheme is becoming dragged out.

The Peterborough scheme is a one-off reclamation, not likely to be repeated. Nor is the C.E.G.B. ever likely to agree to such terms again. For the terms were startling. When I asked the Board for details, they refused, saying 'the normal commercial considerations are involved here and it would not be in the wider interest of electricity consumers – who eventually have to foot the bill – for the comparative disposal costs to be freely available'. In fact, the C.E.G.B. pays for all the transportation, paid for all the necessary buildings and terminals, and pays a small sum to London Brick for each ton of ash it dumps. London Brick even gets a small rent for the C.E.G.B.-built terminal buildings. A startling piece of business acumen by London Brick, but C.E.G.B.'s feelings were indicated by an assistant regional director of the Board, G. W. Blackman, speaking at the Brickfield Conference:

If all interested parties could really get together, we could perhaps arrive at more constructive schemes than has been the case in the past – provided the electricity consumer is not asked to bear more than his fair share of the cost. What would seem to me worth looking at, in some cases, is the total social benefit that could be obtained by using spare power-station ash, as a national asset for land reclamation – and that would involve other parties beyond the electricity consumer recognizing that they must foot part of the bill.

However, an unyielding defence of London Brick's charges and levies on the body that was solving the Brick Company's derelict-land problem was actually made earlier in the same conference by J. P. Bristow. He said,

It may be said, it will be said, that London Brick Company wins all ways, but account should be taken of dislocations to our workings in the area which were inevitably caused by the Electricity Board [sic]. New roads have to be constructed, haulage roads moved, waterways diverted, pumps re-sited and, whilst the Electricity Board paid for most of that, the whole scheme has to be watched carefully so that there is no interference with production.

The sheer red-necked rigidity of that statement, its stone-wall refusal to recognize the company's duty to restore, takes my breath away. It is one of the most die-hard utterances by a British industrialist about the environment I have ever come across.

Since that Brickfield Conference London Brick's attitude has not changed substantially. 'We're in business to make money in this operation, too,' says Jeremy Rowe, London Brick's deputy chairman and managing director of the Peterborough scheme. 'There's money in reclamation just as in old days there was money in dereliction.' London Brick is at least consistent. Most other suggestions for reclaiming the pits have been asked to jump the same hurdle or have run into technical snags. One very plausible idea is to use them as reservoirs. It's attractive – reservoirs like Grafham Water provide both water and pleasure to the yachtsmen and fishermen. Reservoir pits, however, have one main problem to overcome: the sides of a worked out brick-pit are too steep after the drag-line excavators have hauled their last loads; water levels in a reservoir fluctuate as people turn on or turn off their taps, and the almost vertical pit sides would be highly unstable. So the sides would have to be sloped to an angle of about one in five, and some lining of side face, probably with hard-core, would be necessary. Such sloping requires massive amounts of land and money: the size of the pit is enlarged by the earth moving, bringing further problems. London Brick has been given by the Great Ouse River Authority a figure of £1·3 million as a stabilization cost of one pit near Peterborough that would have a potential storage volume of nearly four hundred million gallons. Improbably, it is cheaper to provide water and dig a new pit than to adapt an existing one. The river authority estimates that the unit cost of the Peterborough pit would work out at £3·35 a thousand gallons, compared to £0·75 a thousand gallons for a newly dug reservoir of equivalent capacity, and requiring a nine-acre site.

Both London Brick and the river authority have advanced the commendable idea of so digging the pits initially that they are ready for water use when worked out. The notion so far has come to nothing. No agreement has been made with the river authority, which says the idea is 'all very much in the future'. The same fate befell another London Brick suggestion that the river authority only half-fill a pit, much cheaper on stabilization. The company can be excused delaying restoration of two Bedfordshire pits because of reservoir schemes.

The same fate has befallen also an ambitious plan that would have greatly minimized the derelict land problems in two counties: a shift of the colliery waste from Nottinghamshire mines to the empty clay pits in Bedfordshire: the scheme foresees a colliery slag merry-go-round of trains. Both counties have collected much more than their share of derelict land. Nottinghamshire has a spoil tip for every Bedfordshire brick chimney (about 100 in all), and about 3,000 acres are buried under conical tips or the newer vast ridge tips, dominating industrial villages in the county. By the end of the century eleven square miles of the county's surface will be buried, estimates the county director of planning, H. J. Lowe. Some thirteen million tons of waste are dug out of the East Nottinghamshire Coal Field, one of the richest in Britain.

As mines in Scotland and Durham have closed, miners have migrated to Nottingham for fresh work. The mines are linked closely with the ranks of Trent-side power stations. The county is faced with a growing spew of waste, and less and less space to place it on.

Nottinghamshire county authorities have carried out imaginative schemes with tips, particularly in re-shaping them into natural features and then seeding them. But the waste still comes. The Bedfordshire merry-go-round was put forward to take care of it: a suggested three to four million tons a year, dumped in the pits and sometimes over the pits, so that small hills could be built into flat, dull Brickfield Valley. The scheme foundered, to the frustration of Lowe of Nottinghamshire, who pleaded for it eloquently at the Brickfield Conference. It now gathers dust on the files for two reasons. For finance the scheme clearly needed a sharing of the cost between London Brick, the National Coal Board and the government (on behalf of the people who have so benefited from the products of the two counties). British Rail did its sums and calculated an annual average charge of 72½ pence per ton to shift the spoil south ninety miles. But London Brick would not pay its share of the bill; the government would not pick up its third, probably on the grounds that the dereliction in the two counties does not qualify for aid, under the lunatic definition of derelict land in the grant-aid regulations. The special government aid for the merry-go-round was not offered. The county had to drop the idea.

The other problem was the scale of muck-shifting. Spoil would have had to be delivered at the rate of twenty train loads a day, each train filled with 1,000 cubic yards, six days a week for thirty years. But this problem is not insuperable: immense progress has been made conveying spoil pipelines; some carry waste vast distances, such as a pipeline which runs 275 miles to deliver coal to a power station at Black Mesa, in California. The cost could be as low as 20 pence a ton. Such a pipeline should be constructed as a matter of urgency but it will require a tripartite agreement to meet the cost. London Brick no doubt would have to be brought unwillingly to the cash register. E. H. Burton, the company's estates' manager at London Brick, was asked what the company was doing in 1971 on the question of colliery spoil. 'Are we looking at it? I expect the people with the problem to be looking at it,' he replied.

On occasion, London Brick gives signs of a dawning enlightenment. In 1970 the company started negotiating the handing over of a 245-acre water-filled pit known as Stewartby Lake to the county council, charging a peppercorn rent of £50 a year. Together with the Countryside Commission, the county council is hoping to convert the lake into a country park, to include a sailing club with mooring space for 750 boats, parking for 1,000 cars, children's play facilities, paddling pools, picnic areas and so forth. Projects like Grafham Water, the new reservoir in Huntingdonshire, which is vastly over-subscribed by sailing clubs, have shown how successful such projects can be.

Tree-planting schemes – partly to hide eyesores – are also being taken up with more enthusiasm by the company. Up to 1970 the company had planted 50,000 trees in the period since the war – not a considerable total. Many of these trees died, perhaps because of alterations in the water table, perhaps because of air pollution. A new approach to tree planting was indicated in late 1970 when London Brick and the county council agreed to provide fifty acres in the brickfield for the experimental planting of 50,000 trees over a five-year period. The idea is to find out what types of trees grow best in the brickfield and whether they can be grown as economic plantation crops. The cost is being split three ways: between London Brick (50 per cent), the Countryside Commission (37·5 per cent) and the county council (the remainder).

It is a delusion, however, to look on such projects as the central restoration problem. This key question – the filling of the pits – is simply bedevilled by the cash nexus. The benevolence of the Stewartby Lake scheme will not be the pattern for all London Brick's recreational projects. The new rubbish-recreation subsidiary, London Brick Land Development, is looking to see what can be made out of visitors to restored pits. It is considering amusement parks, miniature roundabouts, water-skiing. 'We've got to do something that pays,' says Rowe. 'How does Woburn Abbey make a profit?'

Nothing succeeds like success; yet if London Brick do succeed in selling re-vamped pits to a leisure-happy public, the company will *not* have demonstrated a new approach that at once beats pollution and pleases the cost accountants. Restoration must be done, not at the whims of supply and demand and market forces, but as an integral part of an excavation project, whether it be sand, gravel and roadstone, china clay or chalk. Planning permissions for future excavations must require complete restoration to a purpose, at the necessary cost. Companies must internalize, include, restoration costs at the outset of the project. In future no organization must be allowed to dig and despoil, and leave restoration to the future to solve.

Chapter 6

Parks for Peace

The first propagandist for national parks in the wild places of Britain was William Wordsworth. The poet pleaded, in a peerless statement of the case for preservation in the Lake District, that the lakes should be looked on 'as a sort of national property, in which every man has a right and interest who has an eye to perceive and a heart to enjoy' (*Guide through the District of the Lakes*, 1835). The Victorians were great park makers; many British cities owe green open spaces to Victorian planners. Their motive was primarily to offer 'a decent and respectable entertainment' to the urban-worker family, in place of the grosser pleasures of Gin Lane. But Wordsworth took matters much further than his contemporaries. He advocated as necessity that the wilderness should be kept wild and undeveloped; he felt that all people should have the chance to renew, to re-create, themselves. He placed a special value on wild nature itself, believing that there is a richness in a man being moved 'spiritually' by natural things and that there is a limit to the amount of emotional stirring a floral display in lawn bedding under a city sky can accomplish. He placed this value above the rights of the property owners in the District.

William Morris expressed another motive for national parks in 1887 when he wrote: 'Our towns must not eat up the fields and the natural features of the country; nay I demand even that there be left waste places and wilds in it, or romance and poetry – that is Art – will die out amongst us.'

From Wordsworth and his time onwards, the national-park campaign has been fuelled by radical motives: concern for nature combined with an anxiety for people who lived their lives in mills and mines, in a foul air and a vista of mean back streets. This sentiment has fuelled the campaign for national parks from its beginnings. This book has examined what has been happening to the fresh water, the air, the sea and the land amidst which people live. It has tried to report upon what has been and is occurring, and the findings have been unpleasant. The air is being inadequately protected by the Alkali Inspectorate; rivers and estuaries are grievously polluted; derelict land is increasing at a greater rate than it is being restored; noise levels are rising; the sea has been grossly misused. A real irony exists then when we look at what is happening in our national parks, which were created as places where ordinary people could escape the harsh environments in which they live and work, places where industrial pollution could be forgotten. Yet we find that the national parks today are being subjected to wide-scale industrial exploitation, and that the government, in the name of its people, is actually rendering economic by grant aid the sacking of the parks by industrial corporations. The wild places, the bolt-holes, are being raided.

The crucial stages in parliamentary initiatives for national parks have all come from Labour governments. The first Labour Prime Minister, Ramsay MacDonald, set up the first official inquiry into the feasibility of creating national parks – 'with a view to the preservation of the natural characteristics including flora and fauna and to the improvement of recreational facilities for the people'. The inquiry gave fruit to the Addison Report in 1931, which stressed that it should be made easier for pedestrians to get into areas of natural beauty. This democratic theme was taken up later by the famous *National Parks* report by John Dower in 1945. Of rambling and grouse shooting Dower said: 'When the issue is seen as a broad question of principle – whether the recreational needs of the many should or should not outweigh the sporting pleasures of the few – there can be little doubt of the answer: that walkers should, sooner or later, be given freedom of access over grouse moors.'

Dower passed on the baton to a committee under Sir Arthur Hobhouse, which reported in 1947 that the countryside should be a national playground, for air and exercise, for the 40 million urban dwellers of this country. It disapproved strongly of notices reading 'W.D. Danger Keep Out' or 'Private' or 'Trespassers will be prosecuted'. 'As the urban dweller fought in the past for his urban commons and open spaces,' it said, 'so he and the country man need today to agree together how best to achieve fuller public use of the countryside through footpaths and access to uncultivated land.' Finally it was the post-war Labour government that passed the National Parks and Access to the Countryside Act in 1949. Sentiments expressed on the Labour side of the House of Commons accorded with Anthony Greenwood, who said in debate,

I remember that the Liberal Party used to say 'God gave the land to the people', but I want the people to enjoy that land as a right. I do not want the women in my constituency who work in the weaving sheds, and the men who work hard, to be allowed to go on somebody else's open country as an act of grace or privilege conferred by the landowners ... I hope that we shall abide by this principle so that the working people of this country can enjoy fresh air and quiet as a right and not a privilege.

The ten national parks in England and Wales, in short, are children of the Labour movement. They were created for the people of these countries as a permanent heritage – places of escape and renewal for successive generations of townspeople suffering from urban living. Their creation was one of the more civilized and dignified actions of Parliament in this century. Yet this bequest has always been severely at risk, and it has entered in the 1970s its most testing time. This was signalled by a decision in mid 1971 by the Department of Trade and Industry to finance the costs of mining corporations in exploring the rock strata of Britain for minerals. The Government pledged itself to pay thirty-five per cent of a mining company's exploration and feasibility study costs. Initial funds of £25 million were fed into the scheme, with provision for a further £25 million if necessary. 'The scheme', commented the *Daily Telegraph* city page, 'should be a great incentive for companies to turn Britain into a new Western Australia.'

A Trade and Industry spokesman announced that around a hundred companies from all over the world had approached the department and that at least thirty were then actively prospecting in various parts of Britain. The Minister for Industry, Sir John Eden, told the Commons: 'This country has considerable potential for mineral development and we have been considering how to encourage mining companies to prove our mineral resources so that they can be used to the best advantage.'

By geological mischance, this 'considerable potential' is lodged in the upland areas of Britain, the wild and natural places too rugged for any past exploitation but deforestation followed by simple hill farming and small-scale mining. Metal-bearing rocks are old rocks, the basic component of the national parks. Younger, carboniferous formations are in the lowlands of Britain. Many small mines sunk shafts into the uplands; first the Romans, and then exploiters in the eighteenth and nineteenth century. Today the deposits of high grade ore are exhausted.

These old mining haunts are now being examined not by forty-niners with picks and washing pans but hydra-headed international corporations with the most modern seismic instrument and aerial surveys. The new miners have been encouraged by a number of factors. The Department of Trade and Industry, (the exploitive half of the government) is aware that it costs about £600 million a year to import non-ferrous metals like copper, tin, lead and zinc, and barium minerals (used as paper and cloth fillers), fluorspar and potash for fertilizers. The savings in foreign exchange might be considerable. The government has been nervily aware that Britain cannot control her overseas sources of metal as once she could. Zambia, the largest copper-exporting nation, is displeased with Britain's arms shipments to South Africa; in July 1971 Chile, the second largest copper exporter, nationalized its copper industry, to the discomfiture of the American companies, Kennecott Copper Corporation and Anaconda Copper Company. New hard bargaining by the Middle East oil suppliers has also shaken Western nations into a realization of the degree of their dependence. A domestic supply of copper, in politically stable Wales or Scotland, considers the department, has attractions.

The mining corporations themselves now find the British ores more palatable. New techniques of mining enable ores to be extracted in concentrations that once would have been hopelessly uneconomic. Before the Second World War metal concentrations much below 1·2 per cent were not mined. Now concentrations of

0·4 per cent are exploited. Rio Tinto-Zinc, the huge international mining corporation, has a highly profitable open-cast gold mine at Palabora in north-east Transvaal, South Africa. The gold content is about 0·5 per cent of the rock, which is torn up by giant excavators and bulldozers. The ores in the British rocks, like the Harlech Dome in Snowdonia, are around this percentage. With government aid served up and a cheek-by-jowl access to the markets, the national parks are potentially profitable mining areas.

The threat is not a new one. That very first government report on national parks, by the Addison Committee in 1931, stressed quarrying as a serious disfigurement.

John Dower in his superb 1945 report put the exploitation cost most forcibly of all. 'Damage,' he said,

has come and may come from quarrying and mining, with their trail of waste-heaps and polluted streams, and in some cases of associated industrial plants; from large-scale afforestation, blanketing the varied colours and subtle moulding of the hillsides with monotonous sharp-edged conifer plantations; from ill-considered felling of woodlands, of hedgerow timber of amenity value; from dams and other works of water supply and hydro-electric undertakings, particularly where these convert natural lakes into artificial reservoirs with large rise and fall and consequently unsightly margins; from the poles and pylons of electricity distribution; from the cruder forms of drainage and embanking operations; from military occupation, especially in the permanent artillery tank and bombing ranges; and from unnecessary or unsuitable road 'improvements' in wide variety – new routes, widenings, bridgeworks, car parks and discordant urban types of surfacing, fencing, signposts and other 'furniture'. (H.M.S.O.)

It is possible to draw up a list, not exhaustive, of depredations on or threats to individual national parks.

Dartmoor National Park

The park includes some of the huge Lee Moor workings of English China Clay Ltd, the principal clay miners in Britain. Large areas, both in and on the edge of the park, are composed of clay pits, clay waste tips, or lagoons for disposing of micaceous resi-

due. The devastation is gross, and the white sand tips are visible
for many miles. The company sought planning permission in
1971 to use more areas at Lee Moor to mine and dump waste. As
this book went to press, the result of the three-month planning
inquiry had not been announced.

A reservoir to supply north Devon's estimated water needs in
A.D. 2000 is under construction at Meldon in north Dartmoor –
in spite of the planning inspector's recommendation at the public
inquiry that the valley be spared for its exceptional beauty. In
central Dartmoor the Water Resources Board recommended the
building of a reservoir at the heart of the moor at Swincombe to
provide water for Plymouth and south-west Devon. Heeding the
advice of national and local amenity organizations, a House of
Commons Committee decided in December 1970 that the pro-
moters had not made a case, and stopped proceedings. Since then
a new campaign to put a reservoir down at Swincombe, consuming 745 acres, has got under way.

Disfigurement of areas by granite and millstone quarrying
also exists. In 1971 Western Alluvials Ltd approached the local
authority for permission to prospect for tin. Ugly conifer plantations have been laid down by the Forestry Commission.

Exmoor National Park
Four reservoir sites are being examined to augment water supplies from the Exe. One site, at Landacre, is in the best moorland
scenery. There would be 'great damage to the landscape', reports
Official Architecture and Planning, March 1971.

Pembrokeshire Coast National Park
Military land and installations take up large areas of the park.
The coastal path sometimes had to leave the cliff edge and go
inland because of military occupation.

Brecon Beacons National Park
Disfigurement by coal mining and limestone quarrying. Plans for
a reservoir at Cefn Fedw Ganol on the Senni were severely interrupted by militant action from farmers in the affected valley. The
plan was eventually abandoned.

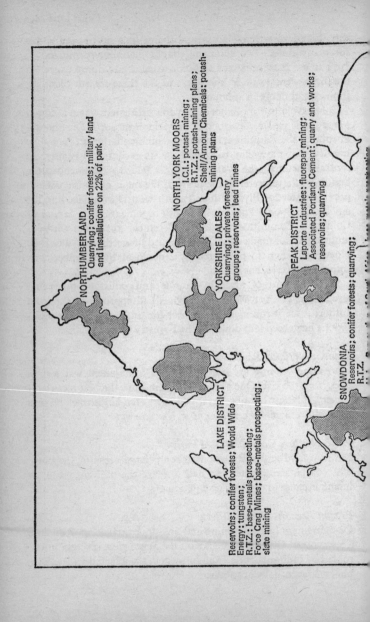

NORTHUMBERLAND
Quarrying; conifer forests; military land
and installations on 22% of park

NORTH YORK MOORS
I.C.I.: potash mining;
R.T.Z.: potash-mining plans;
Shell/Armour Chemicals: potash-
mining plans

YORKSHIRE DALES
Quarrying; private forestry
groups; reservoirs; lead mines

PEAK DISTRICT
Laporte Industries: fluorspar mining;
Associated Portland Cement: quarry and works;
reservoirs; quarrying

LAKE DISTRICT
Reservoirs; conifer forests; World Wide
Energy: tungsten;
R.T.Z.: base-metals prospecting;
Force Crag Mines: base-metals prospecting;
slate mining

SNOWDONIA
Reservoirs; conifer forests; quarrying;
R.T.Z.

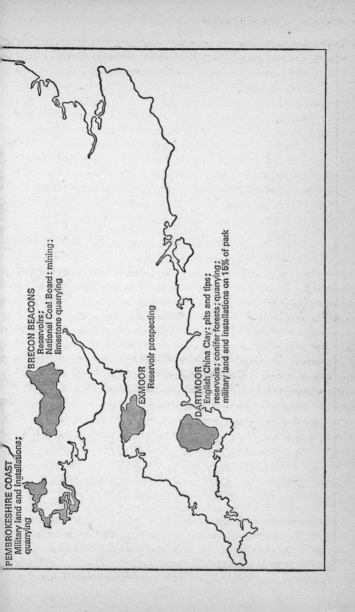

PEMBROKESHIRE COAST
Military land and installations;
quarrying

BRECON BEACONS
Reservoirs;
National Coal Board: mining;
limestone quarrying

EXMOOR
Reservoir prospecting

DARTMOOR
English China Clay: pits and tips;
reservoirs; conifer forests; quarrying;
military land and installations on 15% of park

Snowdonia National Park

Boundaries of the park carefully drawn to exclude some of the worst dereliction by the vast slate quarries and tips around Blaenau Ffestiniog. Disfigurement of valleys caused by reservoir schemes. Reclamations of the Portmadoc area, on the edge of the park, are over 100 years old and their ugliness has not been tempered by age. An outstandingly beautiful area of the park, Coed-y-Brenin, may be the centre of mining activity by Riofinex, a subsidiary of Rio Tinto-Zinc Corporation. At least two other corporations – Union Corporation of South Africa and Noranda-Kerr, a consortium of two Canadian companies – have bought up prospecting rights in Snowdonia.

Lake District

Two fine lake valleys were despoiled by Manchester Corporation: Thirlmere and Haweswater converted into reservoirs, creating a barren tidal strip around the lakes, as water demand fluctuates. Ugly conifer plantations were introduced at Thirlmere and elsewhere by the Forestry Commission. Haweswater may be further despoiled; a subsidary of Rio Tinto-Zinc was granted permission by Manchester Corporation to make preliminary surveys in 1971. The same rights were granted to R.T.Z. by the Forestry Commission at land near Broughton in Furness. Force Crag Mines and Coniston Copper Mines Ltd also survey in the District. There is some disfigurement by slate mining.

Yorkshire Dales National Park

There is quarrying in several parts of the park, extensively at Ribblesdale. Private forestry groups have been involved in plantation controversies especially at Langstrathdale. There were three reservoirs and plans for a fourth. Old lead mines in the Swaledale area may attract new attention.

Northumberland National Park

There is quarrying again and a huge Forestry Commission 'arboreal slum' in the words of John Hillaby, who had to walk through it in his 'Journey through Britain'. The slum actually adjoins the park. Proposals exist for a large reservoir at Kielder.

North Yorks Moors National Park

Three different companies are involved in potash-mining schemes. Cleveland Potash Ltd, a subsidiary of Imperial Chemical Industries, constructing a mine at Ould Boulby near Staithness. Armour Chemicals and Shell (U.K.) have combined to form Whitby Potash Ltd and have been granted conditional approval to mine near Whitby. The refinery site would be just outside the park boundaries, but most of 12,000 acres involved in the scheme would be within. Structures 80 to 130 feet high with a 260-foot stack for waste gases are included. Rail transport would convey 450,000 tons of potash a year. The scheme was not yet taken up by 1971 owing to a fall in world potash prices.

Rio Tinto-Zinc is also involved, setting up Yorkshire Potash Ltd, for a scheme covering some 15,000 acres betweeen Whitby and Robin Hood's Bay. The operational area would be near the coastal section of the Cleveland Way long-distance footpath. Rail transport envisaged to carry about one million tons of potash annually. The scheme in 1971 was not yet taken up.

The North York Moors also harbour natural gas. Home Oil of Canada, in partnership with Gas Council (Exploration) Ltd, were granted permission to sink boreholes at Ebberston Low Moor and Rosedale. Two promising strikes were made; a gathering site within the park of about one and a half acres was constructed, and the gas sent thence to a processing plant outside the park at Pickering. In July 1969 Home Oil of Canada applied for permission to prospect for oil at Stoney Ridge on Westerdale Moor. Permission was refused by the government, partly because it would have involved construction of six miles of new road over the moor. There are huge Forestry Commission conifer plantations.

Peak District National Park

It is host to a number of disfiguring industrial operations. 'Modesty quarries have extended beyond recognition,' says the Park Board. A year before the National Parks Act (1949), Associated Portland Cement received planning permission to build a cement works at Hope Valley. In 1968 the company applied for more land and a new plant. Permission was granted, subject to conditions. Fluorspar is mined from Stoney Middleton Dale, by Laporte Industries Limited. Two tailings dams were constructed near Laporte's treatment plant to hold an ugly yellow waste slurry. In 1969 Laporte applied for permission to build a third dam, taking up seventy-two acres at Blakedon Hollow, at the head of Coombs Dale. Peak Park Planning Board opposed the proposal 'to lay waste a further large area of land'. The board approved the building of a third small dam near the treatment plant, refused an extension of mining at Longstone Edge until discussions with the company on alternative ways to dispose of the slurry than dumping were concluded.

In 1970 the planning board refused permission to allow Hoveringham Stone Ltd to extend quarrying at Bradwell. Enforcement notices were served in 1970 on the company to stop stockpiling and waste tipping at Hartle Dale.

The Peak Park's attractions to mining may be judged by the fact that merely in the year ended 31 March 1971 the planning board had received forty-one mining applications, most of them, of course, minor. Many reservoirs have been constructed within the park – some fifty-five, varying in size from four to 500 acres. In 1970 and 1971 ten new sites were considered for reservoirs. 'Strings of reservoirs in some of the valleys, notably Derwent and Longdendale, overweight the landscape with their insistently artificial effect,' said John Dower in his 1945 report. The planning board has every year to adjudge applications, especially from the Trent River Authority, some of which cause it severe unease.

This incomplete catalogue of reservoirs, mines, lagoons, plants, factories, forests, tips and quarries indicates that the national parks have been a happy hunting ground for industrialists (municipal or private) for many years. The point this makes is to underline how the general intention that lies behind national parks has been frustrated. John Dower concluded his own list of vandalism that the natural wild places have had to bear by saying:

It is not of course a question of prohibiting such uses of land anywhere and everywhere: most of them – though not in any avoidable ugliness or wastefulness of form – are essential to the national economy, and suitable sites must be found for them. But it matters enormously *where* and *how*. In National Park areas, the less of them the better . . . They must be made subject to a control no less effective than that applied to ordinary building development; and, if continuance of uses and works already established must usually be accepted, any new exploitation – or major extension of an existing one – should be permitted only on clear proof that it is required in the national interest and that no satisfactory alternative site, *not* in a National Park area, can be found. Such cases should be rare.

The wartime coalition government did not commit itself to Dower's report when it was published, but the Hobhouse Committee followed his thinking closely when it advocated that any proposed mining must be 'of vital national importance' and 'of proved national necessity'. Unfortunately this did not get written in directly into the National Parks Act (1949). The national parks were given the status of 'white areas', where no substantial development is expected. But three conditions under which mining might be approved in a national park *were* stated verbally by Lewis Silkin, then Minister of Town and Country Planning, during the second-reading debate of the Bill. Silkin said: 'It must be demonstrated quite clearly that the exploitation of those minerals is absolutely necessary in the public interest. It must be clear beyond all possible doubt that there is no possible alternative source of supply, and if those two conditions are satisfied, then the permission must be subject to the condition that restoration takes place at the earliest possible opportunity.'

These three conditions are the crucial minimum if mining is to be permitted in parks at all. Yet only one mining operation that has been permitted in a national park since the 1949 Act and since Lewis Silkin made that speech can conceivably comply with those conditions. Only for china clay could a case be made out, and not a watertight one at that. Yet the mining corporations have arrived, have surveyed and prospected and mined: river authorities have surveyed, prospected and flooded. Why has the defence mechanism of the national parks been so frail?

Much of the blame, as I have indicated, lies with the omission from the National Parks Act of specific bans on mining or other industrial activity in the parks. Secondly, prospective developers have to bring their plans forward to a national-park authority system that could scarcely be worse fitted for its job. All but two of the parks are administered by side-kick sections of the county councils they cover. In single-county parks the system has been to establish a park-planning committee within the county council itself. Invariably this committee has proved to be weak, with no mind of its own, and reluctant to spend money, especially in providing facilities for the people who visit the parks. The parks which fall across several county councils are administered by joint advisory committees, with representatives from each county council. This latter system is to be changed.

That system, said an abrasive report for the Countryside Commission prepared by Sir Jack Longland and published in 1971, is 'a cumbrous, time-wasting and not particularly effective piece of administrative machinery'. Sir Jack advocated the structure suggested by the founding fathers of the movement – each park managed by its own autonomous authority. The evidence for it, he said, was 'overwhelming'. He found it no surprise that the two best-administered parks were those with their own planning boards – the Peak and the Lake Districts. For all-round performance the Peak Board is in a class by itself because it has a planning board of its own, independent of the county councils; it employs its own planners rather than consultants; it has the power to make a precept on the rates of the county councils for funds. As a result the Peak's services for visitors are without rival; Peak publications are excellent; Peak innovations in management of visitors are radical, like the Goyt Valley traffic experiment in which visitors park their cars on the edge of a traffic-free zone and a free minibus service is provided to take them into the valley. The Peak administrators spend much more money than any other park – the only way in which the proper services can be provided. In the seven financial years ending 1970 the Peak Park spent £878,444.

The other park which approached this total most closely was the Lake District with £622,505 for the seven years. This park also gains from having its own planning board, but the measures have not gone far enough – it does not have its own planning staff but shares those of Lancashire, Westmorland and Cumberland. Christopher Hall, secretary of the Ramblers Association, has ridiculed the fact that when the Lake District Board had to put its view on the Keswick by-pass scheme to a public inquiry, it had to employ an outside planning consultant to represent it. The job should have been done by the Cumberland county-planning officer, but the county council disagreed with the board on the scheme, so the planning officer batted for his first loyalty. Hall also pointed out that Dartmoor was ill-served by its administrative structure:

The Dartmoor Park Committee is under powerful pressure to allow conifer afforestation of the moors uplands, thus destroying the scenery for which it was made a national park. But the committee chose to employ as its forestry adviser until recently the director of a major commercial forestry syndicate active in the West Country.

There is only one way out of this mess: establish a single park-planning board for each park, financially and politically independent of the county councils. In 1971 the Conservative Government showed that it lacked the boldness for this change. The White Paper on local government re-organization from Peter Walker, the Secretary of State for the Environment, rejected such a national-park structure, although it had been accepted by the Redcliffe-Maud Royal Commission on local-government reform. The Conservative Government that on the one hand has offered financial inducements to mining companies to raid the national parks has on the other so far ensured that the national parks are ill-equipped to fight them off. No virtue resides in such consistency.

For the immediate future, resistance to the mining corporations will have to fall to the local amenity societies and pressure groups. The odds are stacked against them. For resources the mining corporations draw on funds measured in millions; the societies draw on the collection-box rattle. For personnel the corporations draft employees to work full-time; the societies rely on voluntary labour for the most part. The gradient the societies have to climb is exemplified best by examination of one company in a park – the case of Rio Tinto-Zinc and Snowdonia. (R.T.Z.'s subsidiary Riofinex was in fact involved, but I shall use the name of the parent company in this section.)

A Welsh tenant hill farmer, one Cyril John Jones, was among the very first people to know that R.T.Z. was interested in British minerals. He farms fifty acres at Dolfrwynog Newydd, Hermon, leased off the Forestry Commission, in the spectacular landscape of Coed-y-Brenin, north of Dolgellau. In June 1968 Jones found an R.T.Z. employee on his lands. The man, said Jones, was taking samples of soil in several hay fields without having asked his permission. Jones objected, and was visited by the senior R.T.Z. local officer, Gordon Sharp. After apologizing, Sharp asked if R.T.Z. could survey Dolfrwynog Newydd, Hermon.

R.T.Z. had been attracted to this part of Merionethshire since 1966, when it had begun to study closely the published geological data. Its eye was caught especially by a reference to Merioneth 'turf copper' – a seven-acre peat bog in which the peat was so enriched in copper precipitated organically from the ground waters that in the 1860s the bog was actually commercially exploited. The peat was stripped, burnt in kilns, and the ashes shipped to Swansea for smelting. R.T.Z. recognized that turf copper represented 'a geological anomaly of a very high order' and perhaps indicated that beneath the turf is a previously unknown layer of bedrock, mineralized with copper. R.T.Z. decided to move, and in May 1968 R.T.Z employees started geological mapping, geochemical and geophysical studies over a wide part of the western slice of the county.

So, when Cyril John Jones came across the R.T.Z. geologist in his hay fields, he learnt of the R.T.Z. interest only a month after it had started operations. But the news travelled exceedingly slowly.[1] The Welsh hill farmers are solitary people, some even are Welsh monoglot, and it took many months before news of what R.T.Z. was doing percolated to the county planning officer or the outside world. In January 1969 R.T.Z. started shallow drilling near Capel Hermon; rock cores brought to the surface quickly revealed that copper did exist, and then from May 1969

1. The first national press report of R.T.Z.'s activities, in the *Sunday Times*, did not appear until 27 September 1970.

the drilling operations concentrated on delimiting the exact area where the copper rock lay. By July Gordon Sharp was able to write a report for his company stating that an area of copper mineralization one mile by one and a half miles had been delimited, with copper in average concentrations of about 0·4 per cent. This is both a large area and a workable concentration.

Only one way to exploit this copper is viable and R.T.Z. know it: by huge open-pit mining, in which the top soil and the overburden rock is removed by bulldozers and excavators, the copper-bearing rock exposed, extracted and taken to a near-by crushing mill. Several 100-acre or 200-acre pits probably would be dug to a depth of some hundreds of feet, over a 1,000-acre field. It has been reported that R.T.Z. would need to remove five million tons of rock annually and that waste rock tailings could be tipped to form hills 600 feet high, if necessary, to hide the mine itself. Or the tailings would be trucked or piped out of Coed-y-Brenin to a dumping area. The ore-bearing rock would be transported, probably by truck, initially, to a copper smelter. The mine could be viable for fifteen to thirty years.

It was not till the end of the year that the Merioneth county planners learnt of the drilling. When they did, they told R.T.Z. that planning permission was required. The company were surprised and said they had presumed that such shallow drilling fell under the aegis of a 'general development order', whereby changes in land use are permitted provided that within twenty-eight days the land is restored to its original purpose. Merioneth disagreed. Finally R.T.Z. did apply for planning permission on 28 April 1970. But it continued drilling almost up to the opening date of a public inquiry into just that activity. Merioneth, concerned, had asked the Welsh Office to set off the procedure for a public inquiry, which was fixed to open on 15 December 1970.

Whether or not small drilling rigs mounted on trailers need planning permission is a moot point. Indisputable is the fact that by the time the public inquiry did open, R.T.Z. had under its belt a considerable quantity of geological information. It had drilled in the Coed-y-Brenin area some seventy-two bore holes, and it had rapidly accelerated its drilling after the date it applied for

145

planning permission – forty-eight holes were drilled after 6 April 1970. The public inquiry into whether R.T.Z. *should* drill turned out partly to be an inquiry into whether it *ought to have* drilled.

But the drilling for copper under the farms and forests of Coed-y-Brenin was not at first the sole R.T.Z. interest in Merioneth. R.T.Z.'s exploration assessors, said the company, had also been attracted to the Mawddach Estuary, which is one of the finest estuaries in all Europe. Its beauty seems to have influenced the perceptions of shoals of British writers and poets. In 1824 William Wordsworth described how he 'took boat and rowed up the sublime estuary, which may compare with the finest in Scotland. With a fine sea view in front, the mountains behind, the glorious estuary running eight miles inland, and Cader Idris within compass of a day's walk, Barmouth (the town at the estuary mouth) can always hold its own against any rival.' A contemporary of Wordsworth, Sir T. N. Talfourd, went even further:

The Mawddach Estuary far surpasses in glory even the well-known Rhine. Let anyone who has knowledge of the two scenes call to memory that glorious estuary reposing in beauty and crowned in grandeur; look down its avenue of sparkling light to the distant sea, glistening in the western light; let him glance on the one side at its curving shore of oak sprinkled meadows, edged and broken by rock, and on the other to the pillared precipices of Cader Idris, and then, with all respect to the noble substance of the flowing Rhine, gaze at its vine-spotted banks and say if there is the faintest approach to rivalry.

Ruskin visited the estuary and remembered it. In 1876 he wrote, 'There is but one finer walk in Europe than the walk from Dolgellau to Barmouth, and that is the walk from Barmouth to Dolgellau.' William Gladstone agreed with Ruskin (plagiarizing the remark in a speech) and so have contemporary politicians.

Planning permission for a few new farm buildings on the south side of the estuary was refused in 1969 by George Thomas, then Secretary of State for Wales. He said: 'The amount of undeveloped coastal and estuarial areas in Britain is relatively small and diminishing. The point has been reached where every effort should be made to preserve the finest landscape in these areas in its present state.'

Any would-be developer with a grain of local knowledge would have quickly realized that a plan to mine in the Mawddach would get a reception as hostile as that greeting an oil company applying for planning permission to put a refinery in St James' Park, London. But R.T.Z. told the public inquiry it had become interested in what may lie beneath the estuary: alluvial gold. The river that flows into the estuary has often been diverted into the pans of hopeful speculators. It drains much of the old boomerang-shaped Dolgellau gold belt inland, and in the nineteenth century small-scale panning of the Afon Mawddach occurred intermittently. Even today tourists try their luck in the stream, sometimes emerging with a few pounds (sterling) of gold. R.T.Z. said it was working on a sophistication of the same principle – gold in the hills, gold in the stream, gold beneath the alluvial mud of the estuary. R.T.Z. told the public inquiry that its investigators had panned the small streams flowing into the Mawddach in 1969, and in nearly all cases the panned concentrate showed 'significant gold values'. Depth soundings were carried out and these generally showed that the bedrock would be within reach of huge dredgers. Rumour then quickly got about Merionethshire that R.T.Z. was considering employing four dredgers of Leviathan dimensions – 300 feet long by 80 feet wide by 80 feet high, and floated either in separate lagoons or by flooding the estuary with a barrage. The dredgers would reject massive quantities of mud, to be piled in hillocks, probably above the water level. No one had to be a professional ecologist to realize that such a massive exploitation would do appalling and irreversible damage to the delicate functioning system of an estuary. The existing wildlife, flora and fishlife and drainage pattern would be up-turned and lost. It would be an ecological Hiroshima.

Undaunted, R.T.Z. discussed the matter with the owners of the mineral rights, H.M. Crown Estates Commissioners, and was granted a licence to look for gold in the estuary. Finally it applied for planning permission to drill six prospecting holes from pontoons in the estuary. The application went in together with the Coed-y-Brenin copper hunt. The two applications were discussed and examined, but in terms of emotional impact it was quite clear that the Mawddach was the greater generator. The testimonials from Wordsworth, Ruskin, Gladstone, Sir T. N. Talfourd that I have quoted were produced, plus descriptions from Tennyson and Turner, by a high-flying Martin Thomas, counsel for the 273 objectors of the Mawddach Association. A newspaper reported: 'Apparently they were all in love with the place and Mr Thomas had us half believing that they would be picketing the court room if they were still around.' Yet one month before the public inquiry opened, an appropriately disbelieving journalist had put down a hunch and published it. He had the Machiavellian view that when loud protests would be made at its two mining schemes, R.T.Z. would surrender the dubious commercial prospect at the Mawddach, receive plaudits for its sensibility, and get down to mining copper at Coed-y-Brenin. The journalist was Jon Tinker, environment correspondent of the *New Scientist*; his article appeared in that journal on 12 November 1970. Without ascribing to R.T.Z. a kite-flying tactic, it is enough to record that what Tinker prophesied is exactly what happened. It is important to remember this before going into the details of the public inquiry that opened on 15 December in the tiny assize court of the greystone town of Dolgellau.

Within minutes of the government inspector Charles Hilton starting the proceedings, a crucial difference between R.T.Z. and its opponents was drawn. Counsel for the Mawddach Association, Martin Thomas, rose and made the chasm plain before R.T.Z could open its case. Thomas said that he was sure that the applicants

will be anxious to keep the scope of this inquiry as narrow as possible. I expect my learned friend will be talking about three-inch diameter holes and borings in the Mawddach Estuary. No doubt his case will be that such preliminary investigations will not make any substantial difference to the amenities. So it is my submission that this Inquiry should go beyond the narrow scope of the application itself.

The licences to explore, said Thomas, were in reality licences to extract, and evidence should be heard also on issues of impact on environment, the effect on the holiday industry in the county and so on.

R.T.Z. did not disappoint. Mr Thomas. Its counsel, K. F. Goodfellow, and its witnesses stuck to the narrowest canvas. But the inspector agreed to hear evidence on the broad front and leave the Secretary of State for Wales to decide whether to heed it or not. The effect was that two public inquiries appeared to be held simultaneously in the same hall. R.T.Z. spoke of resistivity techniques of depth sounding and boreholes drilled at 600-feet centres. Their opponents used phrases which tugged at the heart, broke into Welsh, quoted poetry, described dereliction and swore. R.T.Z. called as witnesses two geologists, and one chartered surveyor. The opponents called nature conservators, ramblers, professors of planning, fishermen, 'a lover of Wales', ornithologists, mountaineers and Outward Bound schoolmen. But when one of the R.T.Z. geologists, Keith Greenleaves, was asked if he would agree that the Mawddach was probably the most outstanding in Europe, let alone Wales and the United Kingdom, he replied prosaically: 'It is certainly an attractive estuary. I cannot compare it either with pro or con with estuaries in Europe generally. Attractive, yes.'

Greenleaves's narrow field of competence was stressed by R.T.Z.'s counsel after he had been asked detailed questions about the effect on the ecology of the dredging with the craft 300 feet long, 80 feet wide and 80 feet high.

Q: Mr Greenleaves, perhaps we can just get it clear; you are not a dredging expert?   A: No, Sir.
Q: Nor an expert on wild life?   A: No, sir.
Q: Nor a chemist?   A: No, sir.
Q: Nor a marine biologist?   A: No, sir.
Q: Just a poor geologist?   A: Yes.

Yet Lord Byers, who continued leading the Liberal peers in the House while being director of exploration for R.T.Z., wrote in the *New Scientist* on 3 December 1970:

R.T.Z. policy is crystal clear. We are conservationists. We are also miners. We believe that by harnessing the finest brains in the conservation field, ecologists, landscape architects, chemical and construction engineers together with our own geologists, mining engineers and metallurgists, we can show that natural beauty and mining can go hand in hand but at a cost. If they cannot go hand in hand or the cost is too great to show a profitable venture, we will not undertake it. It is a simple and honest policy.

This declaration was seized on by Martin Thomas. 'Where, sir,' he asked the inspector,

are the finest brains in the conservation field, the ecologists, the landscape architects, the chemical and construction engineers, the geologists, mining engineers and metallurgists who are supposed to show at this inquiry, as I understood it, that natural beauty and mining can go hand in hand? . . . Where, sir, is Lord Byers himself?

Lord Byers, very probably, was at his desk in R.T.Z.'s offices in St James' Square, London, not regarding it within his duty to appear at an inquiry about shallow geological drilling in west Merioneth. He left that to his two geologists, one surveyor.

Dialogue between the two parties on the damage mining would cause consisted of charge and no counter charge. The dredging of the Mawddach, said Professor Joseph Allen, planning consultant to the park's joint advisory committee and Emeritus Professor of Town and Country Planning at Durham University, would disrupt the placid nature of the area. It would put heavy traffic on the roads and intensive activity in the waterway itself; could affect the stability of the river banks; create flooding hazards and seriously prejudice the fishing – especially the migratory fishing in the estuary.

As for the Coed-y-Brenin open-cast project, Professor Allen told the inspector that such an area would remain in a ravaged condition for at least five to ten years. Restoration, even if R.T.Z. undertook it wholeheartedly, would not be complete so that the present generation could enjoy it. Besides, at best it 'will produce an entirely new landscape of unpredictable quality; for example, I understand the faces left by open-cast mining will be from 100 to 1,000 feet high'. R.T.Z., of course, did not call its own experts to counter Allen's judgements.

The anti-miners could not even see how an application to

explore could be judged without assessing the results of exploitation. 'This is not Aberystwyth University College wanting to carry out a geological survey?' asked Watkyn Powell, counsel for Merioneth County Council. An encyclopedia salesman was Martin Thomas's simile for R.T.Z.: 'I say that the salesman should have the door shut in his face and should be told "either you persuade me of the merits of your encyclopedia on the doorstep or you do not persuade me at all".' R.T.Z.'s counsel, K. F. Goodfellow, refuted similar charges, saying it was argued 'that we should not be allowed to find out the facts lest peradventure the facts should show we ought to be granted planning permission to mine ... [that] it was important to see that the facts were not even discovered'. The opponents, said Goodfellow, did not feel they could trust the Secretary of State for Wales to make the right decision on all the facts.

In the fullness of time the Secretary for Wales, now Peter Thomas, looked at the facts and announced his much-postponed decision, a few days after the news of the government's cash inducements to the mining corporations. R.T.Z. was granted its permissions. Thomas's assent was subject to various conditions, a time limit, restrictions on the number of drilling rigs and the hours they could be operated. Perhaps most important is the penultimate paragraph of the letter from the Welsh Office to Riofinex. In it Thomas made it clear that his assent in no way conveyed any assurance that permission for actual mining would eventually be given. He added. 'It is entirely within your discretion whether you proceed with exploratory proposals in the absence of such an assurance.'

For R.T.Z., it was enough.[2] The corporation was given until 15 July 1972 to complete its probings of the Mawddach mud and the deep rock of Coed-y-Brenin. If either formation yields enough metal, R.T.Z. will start marshalling the arguments for exploiting the Snowdonia National Park. In different disguises

2. The convention whereby an applicant can divide a proposal into separate stages – first exploration, next exploitation – served R.T.Z. well. If the long-term purpose behind the drilling rigs had been on trial, R.T.Z. might have lost. A change in planning law is now necessary to prevent proposals by instalments.

the same arguments will be advanced by other corporations to exploit other minerals in other parks. It may be as well to examine their validity now, at the start of resurgence of mining in Britain.

The unlovely term 'cosmeticize' is at the kernel of one of the arguments: that restorative techniques are sufficiently advanced to make long-term mining damage a thing of the past. The corporations are taking it seriously. Seven of them last year set up and financed an 'independent commission' on mining in Britain and the environment.[3] The commission, chaired by Lord Zuckerman, includes eminences such as Max Nicholson and (a latecomer) Sir Jack Longland. Among their tasks is

to examine the relevant problems of exploration, mining, continuous rehabilitation and subsequent reconstruction of sites and to make recommendations designed to reconcile economic and technical considerations with other requirements of national policy, especially those concerning physical planning and the environment in terms of amenity, recreation and scientific and historical interest.

The commission was expected to report in the summer of 1972.

Its objects are seemingly laudable. Some minerals must be dug, and where they are dug full restoration should be a condition in every planning consent. Scars of industrial landscapes can be healed only by committed programmes of restoration. But national parks are a quite different case. Most of the mining corporations have their surveyors and prospectors working in the wilderness of Britain, and the implication that mining can be harmonized with *these* environments may be baulked at. It is here that, however expert and well-intentioned the commission's recommendations may be for minimizing the damage of excavators and waste tippings, people can take objection. Wilderness cannot be restored. Once wild country has been industrialized on the scale now threatened it will never be wild again. At Coed-y-

3. The participating companies are Rio Tinto-Zinc, American Metal Climax Inc., Charter Consolidated Ltd, Consolidated Gold Fields Ltd, Noranda Mines Ltd, Selection Trust Ltd and Union Corporation of South Africa Ltd.

Brenin, for example, R.T.Z. will not be able to re-create the landscape, merely with a different contour. Peaty top-soils, once torn off, cannot remain the same if stacked while mining takes place and then returned. Reliable sources indicated that in fact R.T.Z. may be unwilling to attempt to remake wilderness, but will prefer to import top-soils, give the land a gentle contour and set it out as tamed parkland. The reason is simple: 'restored' wilderness would be a shattered landscape. The Mawddach Estuary, by the same token, could not have been returned to its present gentle mudflats and streams once the mud had been dredged, excreted, and dumped. R.T.Z. might have attempted – if it was really at all serious about mining there, of which there is some doubt – to create a new estuary, perhaps turning it into a reservoir or fresh-water lake that could be used for recreation. With marinas and esplanades such a scheme could have been politically sold to local authorities in the area.

Such selling may never become necessary. On 3 September 1971 a correspondent to the scientific journal *Nature* wrote that in doctoral studies from 1961 to 1964 he had studied sediment data and found that the Mawddach had silted up from a *seaward* drift, rather than a landward. Beneath the Mawddach mud, it can be construed, would be only fool's gold.[4] A few days later R.T.Z. indicated it had called off the Mawddach hunt. Sir Val Duncan, chairman of the corporation, said on television that he had been to the Mawddach and he doubted very much whether R.T.Z. would be able to mine without upsetting the estuary's ecology. He was promptly asked by Sir Jack Longland if he could give that assurance in writing.

Many hours of public time were wasted before Sir Val became so moved by beauty of the Mawddach. It is important in the forthcoming public inquiry into whether R.T.Z. should be allowed an open-pit mine at Coed-y-Brenin that absolutely no good feeling accrues to the corporation for its eschewing of the Mawddach.

Our wild places do indeed have an inestimable value. In a sense the greater the artificial surroundings of our social structure, the greater the necessity for wilderness. Dr Frank Fraser

4. *Nature*, Vol. 233, p. 73. Letter from R. M. McMullen.

Darling in his 1969 Reith lectures puts the case for wilderness so well that he must be quoted. 'The ecologist', he said,

sees the decline of the great natural buffer of wilderness as an element in our danger. Natural wilderness is a factor for world stability, not some remote place inimical to the human being. It is strange that it has been for so long a place of fear to many men and so something to hate and destroy. Wilderness is not something remote and indifferent, but an active agent in maintaining a habitable world, though the cooperation is unconscious.

Perhaps, also unconsciously, mining corporation managers share this fear of the wild. If so, Fraser Darling had in the same lectures a crushing judgement upon them:

The practical man (whom Disraeli said was he who could be depended upon to repeat the mistakes of his ancestors) can remove what is the nation's heritage and the nation's tool to allow the easier passage of some mechanical Moloch.

But custodians of the national parks will have to combat much harder arguments than the restoration claim if the minerals are to stay in the ground. Nor will they have the fine phrases of Fraser Darling to draw upon. They must meet the real, chilling drain of unemployment in the small upland communities, precisely because of their remoteness from industrial centres, unemployment tends to be high in these districts, wages to be low and opportunities also few. Social anaemia in a society with these vistas cannot really be appreciated by people for whom the national parks are places for short visits or, at best, longer holidays in the warm, long days of summer. Villages where the young people leave for the cities when they finish school, where always there is an excess of young children and old people, can be mournful places. R.T.Z.'s Snowdonia operations would take place in an area where there has long been chronic unemployment, around eight per cent, double the Welsh average. Not surprisingly, a half-promise of jobs on the mines has brought local authorities like Dolgellau Rural District Council and national bodies like Plaid Cymru out in support of R.T.Z. The succour of jobs, it can be predicted, will be skilfully deployed by the publicists of the big corporations as the campaign for mining gets up pressure. But the argument needs to be critically examined.

Snowdonia mining may be less relieving to chronic unemployment than some vocal local members of Parliament believe it. During the prospecting, the number of local people employed by R.T.Z. may be counted on one man's fingers. If large-scale mining itself takes place, many more jobs will be on offer. Figures as high as 1,000 jobs for a fifteen-year period have been stated. But modern mining in Snowdonia may provide jobs too skilled for local men, too hard for the chronic unemployed of the area. Modern mining managers and technicians would probably be found in Australia and South Africa more readily than in Wales. The basic labouring jobs, plus lorry driving and bulldozer operating, will be open to the local people. An operation with a life of possibly only fifteen years is not the fuel on which thriving communities are built.

In other parks, however, industries have given jobs and opportunities to the local people. Inhabitants of Boulby and local villages in the North York Moors National Park should gain from I.C.I.'s Cleveland Potash mine. With a minimum life of twenty years and a maximum of fifty, it offers long-term employment to 560 people. Fifty of these will be managerial and 300 odd will be underground miners, some of whom will be locally recruited. Many of the 120 general overground workers and twenty tradesmen, say I.C.I., will be from the neighbouring population.

We must, however, examine the problem of employment in these upland and distant areas more closely. And what we find is a situation that does not accord completely with the promises from industrialists. In the county of Merioneth in the winter months of 1971 there were 747 people unemployed, 143 of whom were women. (This is a rate of 2·13 per cent.) It is not a comfortable figure, and it represents an increase on the figures for 1970 and 1969 and 1968, when there were 660, 541 and 648 people unemployed respectively for the same periods. But it is a mistake to assume that these totals could be cut by introducing large-scale manual-labour operations like mining. For one thing, the effect on the unemployment figures of Anglesey Aluminium's new smelter near Holyhead was by no means as invigorating as its propagandists suggested. Some 712 people – a rate of 4·8 per cent – were unemployed in the Isle of Anglesey in June 1970. A year later, and six months after the smelter went into operation, 1,280 people were out of work, a rate of 8·7 per cent. Part of the reason for this increase, it has been suggested, was the presence of an unemployed band of labouring men left over after the smelter construction was finished.

Against this is the case of the Ferodo factory in Caernarvon, which opened in 1962 making some 700 jobs available. The local unemployment figures were markedly better, probably because most of the labour was gathered from the locality. Again, the employment history of Akroyd Ltd, a pyjama manufacturer's at Bala, is interesting. Opened in 1961, since then it has been always short of women workers; in 1971 one of its managers told me, 'If only we could get more workers, we'd employ them.'

Yet the Cleveland case does not breach the argument for refusing mines in the parks. The crucial point is to insist that, yes, jobs and opportunities must be provided, but environment-degrading mining is not the way to do it. Much of Merioneth-shire's income is derived from tourism – £5 million annually for the county or about £400 per family. The northern counties garner two thirds of Wales's income from tourists. This income is not exported to overseas shareholders; it is passed around the neighbourhood. Efforts must be made to maintain and expand this income, though not to the point that the wilderness, the asset itself, vanishes. Industries that offer sophisticated employment and a product with low transport costs must be greatly encouraged by exchequer grant to settle in the national parks. What the upland communities need above all, one local employment officer has said, is an industry with enough of a technological base to form a link with local technical colleges. Then, perhaps, the sixth-form students can be encouraged to stay, seeing a future beyond their last term at the college. Government offices, where the product is carried in a postman's bag, are ideal for the park communities. To see how serious is this problem, consider the facts that Merionethshire loses between twelve and twenty per cent of its school-leavers immediately and between twenty and thirty per cent one year after school-leaving and up to the age of twenty-five.

A prime necessity for the next radical government must be to examine and conclude ways of ensuring a developing life for the parks people. One essential is to succour the local agriculture, the hill farming which maintains some of the finest landscapes in the national parks. The hill farmers have survived in defiance of the predictions of agricultural economists, but there is an end to the degree of privation they will suffer in return for working their own land. Some government support of the hill farmer has been misapplied; the hill-farming grants have served mainly to destroy some of the finest downland in Britain. Where the hill farmer really needs support is in the price of his sheep and cattle. As the Country Landowners' Association has said in evidence to Lord Sandford's government committee reviewing national parks, without the sheep and the cattle, 'the scenery will materially change, for walls, hedges, fences, woodlands will succumb for lack of proper and timely maintenance and repair'. This is not the case with some of the wildest, most remote areas of the parks but it is true for huge areas. The farming people of the parks have a right to work in their own fields, and government funds must be produced to see that they do. It will be vital to ensure that the Common Market agricultural policy does not in the interests of its own internal consistency make such support impossible. Such government finance is precisely the type of expenditure the parks need – in preference to the subsidies the Conservative government offered the mining corporations in 1971.

The other main plank of the mining corporation's campaign is an anthem called the 'National Interest'. It is deserving of a little cynicism. It is a song, said counsel Martin Thomas, that R.T.Z. will take up at the next public inquiry – on the issue to mine: 'R.T.Z. will sing it in harmony, in descant, in every possible fashion.' Even in that first inquiry at the Dolgellau assize court, R.T.Z. witnesses found themselves irresistibly drawn, well, at least to hum it and mumble it. The song exists in several versions. One has it that copper is a strategic metal. Another is that home-mined minerals will reduce our sterling outflow and conserve our foreign-currency reserves. A third version is that we need a politically stable supply of minerals. Nothing is enormously wrong with these arguments, except for an implicit assumption that economic expansion has an overriding place. A belief that must be demolished is that additional industrial activity is more essential to the national welfare than preservation of the surroundings we live in. It is a piece of cant, proffered time upon time to justify major and permanent disturbances to the environment by short-term exploitations.

Britain's real interest is much wider than the expansion plans of industrial corporations. National parks are immeasurably closer to the long-term social needs of Britain's largely urban population. R.T.Z.'s chairman and chief executive Sir Val Duncan told his shareholders at the annual general meeting: 'Unfortunately, the techniques of exploration have not yet reached the stage when the growing demand for raw materials can be satisfied without selecting for mining, areas that we should prefer to avoid.' But 'growing demand' makes this pressure on the parks and 'areas we should prefer to avoid' greater not less. Ore concentrations that are rejected as uncommercial today will become profitable tomorrow. Mining companies work non-renewable resources in a global economy hungry for more: the National Interest will be the principal tool for ensuring that when the time comes, the parks are plundered.[5]

Snowdonia is as good a place as any to stand and fight. It is within a half-day's car drive of the huge population centre of Liverpool, Manchester, Stoke and Birmingham. (The Peak Park has an even richer catchment area: some 17 million people a year visit it.) 'With the increase in population', argued Professor Allen at the inquiry, 'the need to maintain the scenic quality and ap-

5. Sir Val Duncan at R.T.Z.'s 1971 annual general meeting produced one example of the kind of National Interest appeal R.T.Z. might use if it does seek permission to mine in Snowdonia. 'It is pertinent to point out', he said, 'that should Coed-y-Brenin turn out to be an important producer of copper ore, this would be a key factor in the establishment of a copper-smelting complex, at some suitable location in this country. It is anomalous to say the least that no such complex exists in a highly industrialized country like Britain consuming as much copper as we do.'

parent remoteness for which the parks were established becomes progressively more desirable.'[6]

Recent research has shown that when the national motorway network is complete there will be a 32·5 per cent increase in the population for whom a national park will be within a three-hour drive (Richard Jackson, *Area*, No. 4, 1970).

Allen struggled to find an analogy for the mining in the park; he chose eventually to compare the beauty of Snowdonia with the paintings and sculptures in the national collections. 'Clearly', he said, 'destruction of these treasures would never be permitted merely to facilitate an improvement in the monetary situation of the United Kingdom.'

That parallel is imperfect because paintings and sculptures have an exact market value that can be ascertained or closely estimated. Hence the fact that our art galleries are guarded with the most modern anti-burglary devices and the full sanctions of the law. Values of Snowdonia and the other parks, sadly, are much harder to quantify. Hence they are vulnerable. Security guards do not patrol their boundaries; burglars may have thirty-five per cent of the costs of casing the joint paid by government, since economists can readily provide calculations of the benefit to our balance of payments of an indigenous copper mine and smelter complex. The ultimate absurdity of this fact of life is the Mawddach proposals, where sound economic arguments can be advanced for destroying a peerless estuary to extract a metal that is virtually useless except for an artificial value placed on it by an eccentric international money system.[7]

To make sure that Britain's philosophy of physical planning in relation to economic growth is decided upon by the nation and not determined by piecemeal planning applications, the government should set up a study into the cost-benefit value of national

6. An uncouth version of Cymru Ambyth (Wales for Ever) has it:
'Wales was Wales when England was a pup.
And Wales will be Wales when England's etten up.'
England *is* being eaten up.

7. Martin Thomas, counsel for the Mawddach Association, spoke of gold's uses at the inquiry: 'You cannot eat it, you cannot wear it, you cannot burn it, you cannot obtain power from it, you cannot obtain heat or light from it.' But you can store it away.

parks. The fact that the Roskill Commission's calculations on the Third London Airport were criticized and its recommendations ultimately rejected does not mean cost-benefit study has been discredited. On the contrary, the Roskill calculations ran into trouble because they under-estimated the value of the inland environment. The crowded South-East of England has grown to dislike the side-effects of air transport growth so vehemently that it was politically possible only to site the new airport out of England. The Foulness mudflats, washed twice a day by the sea, are as near this as you can get. A national-parks cost-benefit study would examine the real value of the parks and the real cost of mining. It is a rational, democratic method of determining policy. Best of all, it might ensure that 'National Interest' no longer is the anthem only of the joint-stock companies, the international corporations, and the Department of Trade and Industry.

Conclusion

The preceding chapters have indicated that in major respects the surroundings in which many of the British people live are degraded or threatened with degradation. Industry's pollution of the air is inadequately controlled by the Alkali Inspectorate, and while great progress has been made in improving rivers and estuaries, there are fearful barriers to be overcome before the task is completed. The seas around our coasts are suffering major and continuing assault; damage done by persistent dumping of wastes may be limited by swift international action, but damage done by oil – from tanker collisions or the fall-out of hydrocarbons from the atmosphere, initiated by motor-vehicle exhaust emissions – is immeasurably harder to prevent. Advantages of an oil-based growth economy may in even the medium term be found to be outweighed by its side-effects, like seas declining in fertility and value.

The campaign against noise in Britain is perhaps a better feature of the 1970 Conservative administration's performance in protecting the environment. In October 1971 the Department of the Environment announced new restrictions on vehicle noise to a public that had repeatedly been told by the motor industry that further improvement was almost impossible. From 1 April 1973 cars coming off the production line will have to emit no more than 80 dBA; new heavy lorries must meet a limit of 89 dBA from 1 April 1974. These are tighter limits by four and three dBA respectively. A sensible approach is being taken to the problems of aircraft noise and especially of airport siting. But industrial noise – the most damaging of all the exposures people have to bear – is likely to continue to deafen more generations of workers until machine makers are *required* to design equipment to conform to standards. And, sound though much governmental action against noise is proving to be, it is quite probable that more people will be subjected to more noise as more cars come on to the roads and more aircraft need to use our airports. We may be winning battles but losing the war against noise.

As for the land itself, the praiseworthy government programme to attack derelict land is outweighed by more and more acres laid waste every year. And the last wild places are being rendered economic for exploitation by government grants of up to £50 millions to mining corporations with assets of millions.

By and large I have limited myself strictly to what has been happening within Britain and its coastal waters, but the causes of environmental events in Britain are international, not insular. They are the products of methods of industrialization and policies of expansion in both the capitalistic West and in the production-orientated state-socialist nations of the Eastern bloc.

When Samuel Coleridge visited Germany in 1800, he was moved enough about an industrial-pollution problem to write:

> The River Rhine, it is well known,
> Doth wash your city of Cologne;
> But tell me, Nymphs, what power divine
> Shall henceforth wash the River Rhine?

Yet the Rhine that Coleridge saw was as clean as a trout stream compared to the river today, which conveys the industrial wastes of the Swiss and German chemical companies and the sewage of millions. It serves to float dump tankers heading for the sea with cargoes of spent caustic and polyethelene. Accidents happen to it that devastate its whole length, as in 1969, when fish in most of its course down river from Switzerland died. It is heated up, overfed, and deoxygenated.

The Rhine has suffered, along with the environments of all European countries, under the processes of economic expansion and new technology that have so raised the standards of physical living in those same countries. The unmistakable indications now are that economic growth in terms of G.N.P. is eroding the European quality of life. 'The problem we face', said the Royal Commission on Environmental Pollution in its first report in 1971, 'is how to strike a balance between the benefits of a rising standard of living and its costs in terms of deterioration of the physical environments and the quality of life.' No single

European country has yet managed to strike a balance. Despite its international reputation of cleanliness, the richest European nation, Switzerland, has within its borders the single greatest European environmental catastrophe brewing: the destruction of its major lakes. Fertilizer washed off the Swiss fields, detergents washed down those spotless Swiss baths, hydrocarbons emitted by Swiss cars and then washed out of the atmosphere – these wastes collect in Lake Geneva (Lac Léman), Lake Constance (Bodensee), Lake Neuchâtel and others. Sweden – another prosperous European country – also has major environmental problems, especially with its lakes (contaminated by mercury poisoning) and its sea the Baltic, which (put simply) is dying. Prosperous the Swedes and the Swiss may be today, but this is partly at the expense of their environment. And so it is with Britain. The process is well described by the economist E. J. Mishan, who charges that 'as the carpet of increased choice is being unrolled before us by the foot, it is simultaneously being rolled up behind us by the yard'. Mishan goes so far to consider that the 'disamenities' generated by increased production outweigh the value of 'more cars and transistors, prepared foodstuffs and plastic *objets d'art*'.[1]

Mishan expresses in an extreme manner the fundamentally sound idea that society would be better placed if the sea were cleaner, the countryside less damaged, the towns quieter – even though this might imply the forgoing of, say, colour television, or a private car for each family, or a dishwasher in every house. To take the argument much further, it has required an ecologist, Professor Barry Commoner, of the University of Washington, St Louis, to demonstrate that the problems of increasing populations and high economic-growth rates have been many times exacerbated by another factor: changes in the technology of production. In his recent book *The Closing Circle*[2] he argues that the enormous increase in pollution levels in the United States since the Second World War – an increase he estimates at 200 to 2,000 per cent – cannot be accounted for solely by a population

1. E. J. Mishan, *The Costs of Economic Growth*, Penguin Books, 1969.
2. Jonathan Cape, 1972.

increase of forty-two per cent. Nor can it be traced only to affluence since real per capita income rose about fifty per cent. Nor even can economic growth as measured by G.N.P. provide the full explanation: the growth increase was 126 per cent.

To find the answer, Commoner and a colleague worked through huge volumes of United States government statistics, computing the growth rates of each productive activity. He wrote that the winner of this 'economic sweepstakes' with the highest postwar growth rate is the non-returnable soda bottle, production of which has increased about 53,000 per cent in the twenty-five years since 1946. Second place went to synthetic fibres (up 5,890 per cent); third place to mercury for chlorine production (up 3,930 per cent). Chasing behind are mercury used in mildew-resistant paint, then air-conditioning compressor units, then plastics, then fertilizer nitrogen, then electric household goods.

The losers in the race are as interesting as the winners. Railway freight fell 17 per cent, soap 23 per cent, returnable beer bottles 36 per cent, wool 42 per cent, and at bottom of all, work-horse animal power, down 87 per cent. Time and again, argues Commoner, a technology with a slight impact upon the environment has been driven out by one with an intense, degrading one. Plastics have replaced paper production; trucks have driven out trains, using five times the energy, requiring many times the land surface to operate, and causing six times the environmental pollution. Shirts that once were made from cotton produced by energy from the sun are now made from synthetic fibres, produced from petroleum and requiring artificial heat for production. Always the environmentally hostile product vanquished the environmentally compatible. Companies switched from making soap, which natural processes easily destroy, to detergents, which damage rivers and lakes. Farmers changed from working large acreages with natural manures to smaller acreages pepped up with artificial fertilizer. 'The average American,' says Commoner, 'drives about as twice as far as he did in 1946, in a heavier car, on synthetic rather than natural tyres, using more gasoline per mile, containing more tetraethyl lead, fed into an engine of increased horsepower and compression ratio.' No such statistical survey has been undertaken in Britain but the trend here is clearly similar.

Only one basic justification, says Commoner, exists for this switch in technology: the new way makes more money. The return from detergents is nearly twice as high as from soap; truck and lorry companies make more than freight railways; nylon shirtmakers get a bigger profit than pure-cotton shirt manu-facturers. Put simply, that is the conclusion of Commoner's analysis. It is a brilliant analysis of our misuse of technology, regrettably marred by an underplaying of the role of population increase and economic growth in the looming crisis, caused by overworking finite resources, that faces the world.

One has to ask oneself why new modes of production have proved more profitable than the old. The principal reason is that manufacturers employing the new technologies have not paid all their bills. They have treated the air and the landscape as 'free goods'. While they have met such internal costs as raw materials and the labour bill, they have left to society to pay the costs of pollution. This externalizing of costs, this public subsidy of (usually) private industry has produced what the American bio-logist Garrett Hardin has called 'the tragedy of the commons' – air, land and water being a kind of unfenced common.

The pollution problem can now be set out quite simply: indus-try must 'internalize its present externals' – pollution-control costs must no longer be shirked and passed on to the public in the form of damaged environments.

If the stating of the problem is simple, even sketching the right approach to a *solution* is immeasurably more difficult. We need a case study to illustrate the truth of this. The case of Lee Moor may meet the requirement. Any visitor to the south-western part of the Dartmoor National Park becomes aware of Lee Moor before long. He turns a corner and is faced with huge sugar piles of waste sand, brilliant white on a fine day. Beside them are massive pits, up to a hundred acres in extent, and up to 400 feet deep. The peaty brown of the moor is gone – stripped back to display the white bones of underlying rock. The Lee Moor site is the largest single china-clay working owned by English Clays Lovering Pochin Ltd – a subsidiary of English China Clays Ltd, the largest china-clay company in the world. Since the early nineteenth century, its clay has been shipped and trucked to industries throughout Europe.

The damage English China Clays does to this part of Dartmoor is due to the whole process of extracting the clay: to produce one ton of china clay, as many as eight tons of other material have to be extracted. Most of this material litters Dartmoor, creating the white lagoons of residue and the huge tips that steadily expand.

The boundary of the national park bisects the Lee Moor workings, but much of it lies in the park. In 1971 English China Clays had planning permission to mine in 635 acres of the national park, but it applied also for consent to work or tip on a further 597 acres, of which 305 are in the Dartmoor Park. If English China Clays gets approval from the Department of the Environment, the pits and the tips will continue to creep up the moor, destroying hillsides, ancient monuments, hut circles and burial chambers as they go. The company has elaborate schemes for continuous restoration, culminating in a landscape (some time late next century) of lakes, woods and re-contoured tips. But at least for the next 100 years, Lee Moor workings will be a blot on the Dartmoor landscape.

If these are the environmental costs of Lee Moor, what are its economic advantages, even if only in the short term and on an insular basis? The workings clearly earn shareholders of English China Clays reasonable returns, some of which are reflected nationally in a contribution to a satisfactory national balance of payments. In 1970 more than twenty-three per cent of Lee Moor clay mined was exported, earning more than £3 million. They also provide wages to a fair number – 800 odd – of Devon men in an area which, if not desperate for employment, is thankful for the work. But what of its economic advantages to the larger British society – not simply to English China Clays employees or shareholders? This rests on the use of the product. Some is used in the ceramic industry – about ten per cent. China Clay is also used in the making of rubber, paint, plastics, insecticides and fertilizers. But its principal use – a seventy-five per cent share – is in the making of paper and board.

Paper making employs the clay both as a filling and as coating. Because of its inertness and particle shape, the clay binds well in the cellulose fibres which are the major constituent of a sheet of paper. And since the clay is considerably cheaper than pulp, it both lowers the cost of paper per ton and saves more trees from the woodman's axe. That contribution is, without doubt, environmentally valuable. Clay is also used to coat paper – it improves the feel of paper and makes it a much better printing medium. But this use is of less certain social value: coated papers are used mostly in glossy magazines and publicity material. Indeed English China Clays told the Exeter public inquiry last year that its sales of clay rose and fell with the state of the advertising market. When advertisement budgets are fat, demand for glossy paper is high. Now whether Lee Moor should be mined to provide a smooth surface for soft sells is a dubious point. The real value of glossy paper to a society must surely be extremely limited.

Both value and dross, then, seem to be present in the contemporary uses of china clay: they both contribute to the contemporary economy and damage the environment. So the case of Lee Moor shows how hard it can be to judge whether a particular enterprise – a factory or a mine or a smelter – should exist on the grounds of its social value. And of course one man's social value is another man's extravagance. But the fact that much of Lee Moor is an industrial activity taking place in a national park obviously requires a greater justification. In Lee Moor's case longevity is the excuse. It is not normally a justification of a dubious activity to argue that it is better for having been occurring for many years. Some activities, however, may be partly excused on these grounds, where local economies and social structures – towns and villages – have built up around them, and especially where the damage is primarily to amenity (as in Lee Moor) and not to health. The Lee Moor workings grew from random private workings, not a modern application for planning permission, and more than a century before the national park was created. The important task now with Lee Moor is to ensure that the minimum environmental damage occurs. Partly this is a matter of holding English China Clays to every promise – and more – of restoration that it makes. And partly it is a matter of dispersing sand. The huge tips are composed mostly of waste sand. Many people have asked themselves why more of this sand could not be put to use. They have known that in most parts of Britain sand is expensive, and in many parts also, the landscape is turned over to *extract* sand.

Selling the sand requires principally English China Clays to spend money on developing an artificial aggregate to mix with it, making it commercially more attractive, and for the company and the government to work out a method of financing the sand's transport to the South-East, where sand is in short supply. The Lee Moor case thus shows that a pollution problem will often need a package of solutions, including both new private and government initiatives. And I present it while maintaining my general thesis, that I have pursued throughout this book, that companies should not produce at the expense of the environment.

It might be claimed that this choice of Lee Moor as a pollution case study is a soft option. This would be correct. As a pollution problem, much more tolerance can be shown to the derelict landscape around the pits than could possibly be extended to, say, a lead smelter with a bad discharge or a paper mill damaging a river. But Lee Moor does demonstrate that pollution control is often not a matter of simple alternatives. Pollution problems are complexes of factors that often involve local history, the social reliance of communities, as well as measurable environmental effects. In addition, pollution itself is a matter of degree. Pollution usually occurs only when a substance is present in excessive quantities; below a threshold, its presence may be harmless or even beneficial and essential to life. A degree of phosphate in a river is necessary for a *living* river; too much phosphate and the river is overfed and unhealthy.

Flexibility is thus essential in pollution control. The man whose job it is to check the effluent pipes and smoke stacks of industry must have the latitude, within certain limits, to turn the screw gradually or suddenly. With the major exception of noise pollution, if pollution control was entirely centralized and enforced through flat, rigid standards, three things would result. First, many polluters would find life made easier for them –

across-the-board standards would tend to bring a levelling-down rather than a levelling-up. Thus Britain's membership of the European Economic Community is likely to bring a dilution of pollution-control standards, as regulations are phased to accommodate Italian and French practice. Secondly, in cases where standards *were* levelled up, the new laws would be on occasion misfits. Pollution-control officers might find themselves enforcing water-quality standards designed for a slow, central European river upon a factory beside a short, swift, self-cleaning British stream. Thirdly, if a standard required an eighty-five per cent improvement in emissions, a company would be under no incentive to improve up to ninety-five per cent. Yet it might well have this capability.

Central government, however, can aid the pollution controllers most usefully. Four ways in particular can be itemized.

Pollution Taxes

Britain has been very unimaginative about the scope for pollution taxes. These can yield great benefits for the environment. They could be levied in two ways – on the consumer or on the producer, though primarily the latter should be the target. British Columbia used such taxes creatively when the state decided that the non-returnable bottle was undesirable and imposed a small tax on the sales of all drinks sold in such containers. The economic justification for the non-returnable bottle thus disappeared overnight. One can see great opportunities here. The steady creep of the plastic milk bottle could be halted by a special purchase tax – or a discriminatory value-added tax – introduced at budget time in the normal way. The noisiest motorcycles, the wasteful plastic packaging of supermarkets like Sainsbury's, the most environmentally damaging detergents – these could be discouraged by an imaginative and responsible Chancellor of the Exchequer. Taxes should be imposed on a list of metals, to increase their market price, thus encouraging a more parsimonious use of them and a greater degree of re-cycling.

But by and large the taxes should be levied on the manufacturers, for the good reason that it is they that modern economics drive towards adopting the most harmful technologies. Professor Barry Commoner has called for 'an ecological reconstruction' to rebuild faulty technology along ecologically sound lines. For the United States, he estimates that half its industrial plant needs replacing – at the staggering annual cost of 40 billion dollars for the next twenty-five years. While such a 'reconstruction' would greatly cure the pollution ills of the United States, it would also provoke a severe resource crisis unless it were accompanied by a rigorous re-cycling of materials. But pollution taxes could help us towards both such a re-cycling and such a pollution improvement. Senator William Proxmire, a Democrat from Wisconsin, has advanced the idea of a levy of eight to ten per cent per pound of pollutant added to any waterway. A company that met the standard imposed upon it by the river authority would none the less still have the spur to improve its effluent yet further, if the effluent charge exceeded the cost of new pollution-control equipment needed. It has been suggested that such a levy might be based on the biochemical oxygen demand of any effluent, though this might exclude some pollutants which cause little oxygen loss but none the less damage the waterway. Yet, if such a system were tried, the market mechanism would be operating *in favour* of pollution control. A similar tax levy could be calculated for power-station emissions on the pounds of sulphur dioxide emitted – a change that would encourage the Central Electricity Generating Board to think more about removal and less about dispersion.

Freedom of Information

The people whose job it is to control pollution are sometimes quite content that their work should be shielded from the public gaze, as we have seen with the Alkali Inspectorate. Publicity, however, and information are powerful weapons that ought to be utilized properly. There are sections of the River Pollution Acts and the Alkali Acts that promote secrecy. The Alkali Acts keep secret process and control plans submitted by companies to the inspectorate, but they say nothing forbidding giving information about emissions data. The inspectorate has justified its refusal to let the public know about the emissions of a factory polluting its air by appealing to the Official Secrets Act. But, as Friends of the Earth (the militant conservationist group), the *New Law Journal* and the Anglers' Co-operative have pointed out in a letter to the Secretary of State for the Environment in September 1971, the Official Secrets Act only prohibits the *unauthorized* release of information by a government employee. In short, the Alkali Inspectorate can and should be directed to change its policy and authorize the release of pollution data to whomsoever requests it. After all, in its first report, the Royal Commission on Environmental Pollution said that 'one contribution which Government can make will be to stimulate a wider understanding by the public of the pollution problem and a more active public interest in its control'. For this interest, we need the facts.

The secrecy sections of the River Pollution Acts are officially justified as preserving trade secrets. This excuse does not stand up to examination. Give me a gallon of a factory's effluent, says one pollution expert, and I can tell you his production process. Perfectly true, but any company wanting to find out a rival's production methods could just as well send a man along, armed with jam jars, to the place on the river bank where his rival's effluent disgorges. Samples of the effluent could then be taken and brought back to company laboratories for analysis. The fact is that the value of effluent analysis as a revealer of trade secrets is greatly overstated. The secrecy clauses of the Rivers (Prevention of Pollution) Act of 1960 exist only because industry's pressure groups could get away with a piece of nonsense in 1960 that no legislators would accept today.

. That Act must be amended as soon as possible. But in most other cases of pollution-data secrecy, the government need only issue new directives to their departments. The Ministry of Agriculture, Fisheries and Food refuses to tell the public where highly toxic wastes are dumped at sea and by whom. All it needs is the Ministry to be told to change its practice.

The point of making the data public knowledge is simply that greater pressure can be put on polluters if the full facts about their performances are known. Secrecy aids pollution. Nothing concentrates an industrialist's mind more than the knowledge that he will appear in the *Daily Mirror* tomorrow.

Polluting Britain: A Report

The Burden of Proof

People who strive to protect the environment are hampered frequently by having laboriously to collect evidence that a product or a chemical is doing damage. Usually this means that severe environmental damage must occur *before* it is possible to control the source of the pollution. Britain must abandon this pattern. Gradually we should work towards a structure whereby new effluents and products must be presumed to be damaging until they are proved harmless. Manufacturers must no longer be able to say, 'there is no evidence that we are damaging the water supply'. There must be no more cases like that of P.C.B.s, which were proved to be damaging by the appalling method of looking at widespread natural damage, including the corpses of sea birds. Instead, the kind of cautious, double-checking screening that new drugs are subjected to before a doctor may prescribe them is necessary for new chemicals or new applications of chemicals in a variety of products. A new systemic garden insecticide for roses, to take an example, should be carefully tested for its effects on soil, insects (including bees and natural predators like ladybirds), and other wildlife. River-pollution officers complain that every year brings new, more complicated chemicals in effluents and that there is no satisfactory system for ensuring environmental safety. The government must establish an agency to vet new intrusions into the environment before they occur. This agency, which might be called the Clean Products Council, should be government financed but none the less independent. It should have the power to examine any product it wished for its environmental defects, and could be required to examine any product on the demand of the government, any national or local authority, any society with a membership in excess of fifty people, or by petition of a minimum of fifty people.

Stronger Penalties

A perpetual complaint among public-health inspectors or river-pollution officers is the derisory nature of the penalties for flouting pollution laws. The maximum fine for a firm that ignores the consent standards a river authority impose upon it is £100, under the Rivers (Prevention of Pollution) Act, 1960. The government in 1971 said it would increase these and other pollution penalties. To be effective, the increases should be 100 times the existing fines. Apart from making pollution-control equipment much easier for a works manager to justify economically to his head office, heavy fines would bring down much greater publicity upon companies that transgressed. At the moment, a major company can damage a river severely and find itself mentioned only in the local press. When Fisons – the fertilizer and chemical company – polluted the River Orwell in 1971 and was fined £40 the only mention it received in the national press was a three-quarter inch report at the foot of the 'news in brief' section of *The Times*.

Such changes will greatly assist the pollution controllers. The odds will shift towards more intelligent protection. Yet the most valuable control mechanism of all cannot really be created by an Act of Parliament or a decision taken in Marsham Street, the headquarters of the Department of the Environment: *a right attitude and motivation of the pollution controllers themselves is the lynch-pin of a successful campaign against pollution.* And it is in this area that Britain is ill-equipped. While some of our environment is served by the ideal type of controllers, we suffer from a lack of rigour in other departments, particularly sea pollution and industrial air pollution. The attitude of the Alkali Inspectorate that I have so criticized in my first chapter is endemic in much of the Civil Service. These officials set out to cooperate with industry; sadly, they are often co-opted. Curiously, they do not seem to look on themselves as serving primarily the public – like the alkali inspectors, arriving for confidential meetings with industrial polluters and refusing to divulge information to the public that intimately experiences that pollution. In sharp contrast are many local-authority officers who work in pollution control – but then they are more directly answerable to the public. River-authority pollution staff are also markedly more vigilant than the Ministry of Agriculture, Fisheries and Food staff, who are responsible for the protection of our coastal waters.

The customary defence for the 'cooperation not conflict' policy of many of our controllers rests on two planks:

(a) a tough 'police' approach to pollution would make a land fit
only for lawyers, with the courts cluttered with actions and
prosecutions and

(b) that cooperation is anyway more effective. This defence is
aired at length in the 1971 annual report of the Chief Alkali
Inspector, Frank Ireland. The Chief Inspector went to the
United States for three weeks in December 1970.

He records,

> Since I last visited the U.S.A. in 1965, there has been a stiffening of
> the official attitude towards pollution. Some extremely tough laws are
> being enacted and implemented in a very tough manner with typical
> American thoroughness. There seemed at times to be a disregard of the
> economics of prevention. I also detected a wide gulf between some
> control organizations and industrialists and because of this, recourse
> was frequently had to prosecution to gain enforcement, over 1,000
> cases a year in some local areas. This is far removed from our own
> policy of cooperation.

Ireland went to Philadelphia where he found 'another tough,
uncompromising attitude to pollution control'. He records that
the Philadelphian policy is to treat 'any sub-standard emission,
even accidental or caused by breakdown, as a violation'. People
concerned with pollution control in Britain, who know how
often their rivers are damaged or air fouled by yet another breakdown from the friendly neighbourhood factory, may think the
Philadelphians have something here. Not Ireland. He says:

> Control engineers and inspectors are in and around oil refineries, for
> instance, almost all the time and such works are brought before the
> courts about twice per week. The authorities believe that they will get
> a far better response by legal actions of this kind than they will by
> practising cooperation.

From Philadelphia, Ireland's travels took him to Harrisburg,
capital of Pennsylvania State, which also had no time for 'cooperation'. The State has appointed a 'strike force' of six young
lawyers to use legal procedures to the full. Companies that violate
the pollution laws, including by breakdown, have to make their

excuses to the courts. Factories are required to post 'performance bonds' from which penalties are levied if the factory overruns a pollution-control schedule or fails to meet the standards after commissioning.

Let us bear in mind these facts: the real drive against industrial pollution in the United States has started much later, for historical and economic reasons, than in Britain. The United States is anyway a much larger nation, with a tradition of unrestrained 'private enterprise'. The United States courts are more open to public suit and are more flexible.

In the context of these facts, the American action is both right and appropriate. One does not have to be very imaginative to see that if a large British company were required to 'make its excuses' to a court for a breakdown that caused pollution a dramatic improvement in the reliability of its plant would follow. Sadly, our courts are not flexible enough to allow of excuse making. By the same token, Britain would gain from adapting the Harrisburg system of requiring companies to post 'performance bonds' from which penalties could be levied. The Alkali Inspectorate has an unenviable record of failing to ensure that companies keep to deadlines for new agreed standards. So poor is this record that it even brought complaint from Peter Walker, Secretary of State for the Environment (the *Observer*, 5 May 1971).

The odd thing about the charge that a tough, uncompromising attitude would clog the law courts is that it is seldom if ever advanced as a reason for adopting a gentle approach to crimes against property such as theft. Full police action and lengthy court action is taken as the only reasonable procedure. Yet the environment is a public property immeasurably more valuable and irreplaceable than an individual's possessions; laying waste to a landscape is an activity many degrees more reprehensible than, say, shoplifting, for which the courts are the accepted place for a resolution. Objections to pollution policies that would be determined enough to carry through to the law courts if necessary are founded ultimately on an inadequate appreciation of the social wrong of pollution.

But (to be a little less pompous) such objections are also founded on a faulty understanding of pollution control. Once a new and more rigorous standard was established, little more prosecution would be needed than is occasioned by the obligation to pay taxes. The courts of course do hear Inland Revenue actions, but not in sufficient numbers to clog them and provoke demands for 'cooperation' between the Revenue and the reluctant tax-payers. Some years might be needed for the new pollution standard to be accepted, and during this breaking-in period a certain amount of litigation would probably be necessary. But, once the more uncompromising pollution control has established the new climate, the number of environment actions before the courts could be expected to fall.

In the last analysis, however, it is not even the determination of a pollution controller to take legal action if necessary that really matters. It is rather the man's thinking towards his job and his conception of precisely whom he is serving. What is fondly conceived as British moderation in settling pollution disputes is in reality something else: a collusion between the controllers and the controlled, between the industrialists and the inspectors. Only one group has suffered from this pact: the public. Too many people concerned in environment protection in Britain forget that they exist to serve the man on top of the Clapham bus. What the offensive against pollution needs in Britain is not only new laws, not only new agencies, not only new taxes and new technologies, but new attitudes.

Index

Addison Committee, 131, 134
Agecroft Colliery, 40
Agecroft Power Station, 40
Agriculture, Fisheries and Food, Ministry of, 15, 18, 76–7, 80
Akroyd Ltd, 156
Akzo Zout Chemie, 72–4
Albright & Wilson Ltd, 56, 57
Alkali Inspectorate, 6, 7, 8–16, 19, 22–31, 86, 170–71, 173–5;
  achievements of, 12–14;
  failings of, 14, 15, 16, 17;
  founding of, 8;
  industries scheduled under, 10;
  naming of, 9;
  principles of, 11–12, 173–5;
  prosecutions by, 12;
  reform of, 25, 30–31;
  staff of, 8
Allegro, 84
Allen, Professor Joseph, 150
Alt, River, 42, 48
Anaconda Copper Co., 133
Armour Chemicals Co., 139
Associated Portland Cement Ltd, 139
Association of Public Health Inspectors, 103
Atherley, Professor Gordon, 89, 96
Avonmouth, pollution of, 14–15, 70–71

Barr, John, 17, 97, 113
Beales, Philip, 95
Bealey, A. C. & Co., 39
Belcher, John, 77
Brecon Beacons National Park, 135
Bedfordshire Brickfield, 18, 114, 120
Beighton, J., 7
Berry, Frank, 88, 99–100

Berry v. Stone Manganese Marine, 88, 99–100
'Best practicable means', 22–3, 24
Biggs, Mrs M. I., 28, 30
Biochemical Oxygen Demand (B.O.D.), 33, 37
Blackman, G. W., 125
Bowaters U.K. Paper Co. Ltd, 55–6
Bostock, Hill & Rigby, 78
Brickfields, Bedfordshire, 17–22, 114–21;
  acreage to be worked, 115;
  housing contribution of, 114;
  solutions to, 127–8
Brickfield Conference, 114, 116, 119
Brickfield, Peterborough, 115, 116, 123, 123–6
Bristow, J. P., 116, 118, 119, 122
British Sidac Ltd, 42
Broadbent, Dr Donald, 95
Brown & Polson Ltd, 41
Buckley, Antony, 44, 46, 52
Burns, Professor William, 98
Burmah Oil Co., 41
Burton, E. H., 128
Byers, Lord, 149–50

Cadmium, pollution of, 70–71
C.A.V. Ltd, 101
Cat-Ox process, 20
Central Electricity Generating Board, 40, 123–6
Central Veterinary Laboratory, 18
Civic Trust, 113
J. Chadwick & Sons, 47
Chemicals for the Gardener, 77
Channel, Shipping in, 82–4
Clean Rivers (Estuaries and Tidal Waters) Act, 1960, 35, 49

Cleveland Potash Ltd, 139, 154–5
Closing Circle, The, 163–5
Clyde, Firth of, 59
Coed-y-Brenin, 138, 144–54
Coleridge, Samuel, 62
Commoner, Professor Barry, 71, 163–5, 170
Coon, Richard Thompson, 28
Countryside Commission, 128–9, 142
Cowley, Geoffrey, 18, 19, 114, 116
Croal, River, 39
Croda International Ltd, 57
Croft, John, 58, 64
Crossfield, Joseph Ltd, 56
Cutler, Edgar, 3, 8

Darling, Sir Frank Fraser, 153–4
Dartmoor National Park, 153, 158, 165, 166
Davies, Edmund, 15
Davyhulme, sewage works, 47
D.D.T., 61, 76–7
Deafness, noise-induced, 89–92
Decibels, scales of, 87
Derelict Britain, 113
Derelict Land:
    false definition of, 112;
    government plans for, 112;
    growth of, 113;
    national acreage of, 113
Dower, John, 131, 134, 140–41
Dumping at sea, 61–7, 72–82
    European business in, 62, 72–4, 75;
    control of, 62
Duncan, Sir Val, 153, 158
Dundee University, Department of Occupational Medicine, 87

East Lancs. Paper Mill, 39
Economic growth, dangers of, 162–3
Effluent Services Ltd, 66, 79
Electric Power Storage Ltd, 40
Ellesmere Port, sewage of, 49;

refineries of, 56
English China Clay Ltd, 134–5, 165–8
Environment, Department of:
    river-pollution survey of, 34, 35;
    river pollution strategy of, 48–9;
    derelict land, policy of, 113;
    national parks, policy of, 143
Esso Petroleum Co. Ltd, 41, 99
Exmoor National Park, 135

Fisheries Laboratory, Burnham-on-Crouch, 67
Fisons Fertilizers Ltd, 173
Fisons Industrial Chemicals Ltd, 54, 57
Forestry, affects on landscape, 134, 135, 138, 139
Forestry Commission, 135, 138, 139
Freshwater Fisheries Laboratory, Pitlochry, 67
Friends of the Earth, 171
Friends of the Lake District, 44
Fluorine, 18–22, 27–8
Fluorosis, 18–19

Gladstone, William Ewart, 146
Glasgow Corporation, dumping by, 64
Goodman, Gordon, 15
Gowy, River, 33
Grafham Water, 126
Granox Ltd, 53–4
Grasshoff, Dr Kurt, 66
Greater London Council, dumping by, 63–4, 66–7
Great Ouse River Authority, 126
Griffiths, Eldon, Parliamentary Under Secretary of State for the Environment, 57

Hall, Christopher, 143
Hallen, 14
Hanson, Dr Robert, 14
Hardin, Garrett, 165

Heavy-metal pollution, 14, 15, 60, 70–71;
  at Avonmouth, 14–15, 70–71;
  at Swansea, 15–16;
  in marine life, 67–8, 69, 70
Hobhouse, Sir Arthur, 131, 141
Holden, Dr Alan, 67
Holdgate, Dr Martin, 68–9
Holland, Ian, 79
Home Oil of Canada, 139
Hoveringham Stone Ltd, 140
Hudson, John, Ltd, 66, 71, 74–8
Hudson Stream, 74–8

Imperial Chemical Company (I.C.I.), 57, 139, 155
Imperial Smelting Corporation, 15
Industrial air pollution:
  policy on, 11–12;
  standards of, 24–36
Industrial Welfare Society, 92
Institute of Water Engineers, 44
Ireland, Frank, chief alkali inspector, 8–11, 22, 23, 24, 25, 26, 27, 174
Irk, River, 40, 47
Irwell, River, 38–41, 47;
  improvement in, 47

Jackson, Richard, 159
Jeger, Mrs Lena, 34
Jenkins, Dr S. H., 77
Johan Hjort, 72–3
Jones, Cyril John, 144

Kennecott Copper Corporation, 133
Kinder, 66

Lake District, 130, 138, 142–3
Lancashire County Council, 111, 112
Lancashire and Western Sea
  Fisheries Joint Committee, 58
Laporte Industries, 58, 140
Lee Moor china-clay works, 134–5, 165–8
Little, E. A. J., 95

Liverpool:
  water needs of, 43–4;
  sewage of, 52, 57
Loftas, Tony, 62
London Brick Co. Ltd, 19–20, 26, 114–29;
  manufacturing methods of, 116–17;
  attitude to restoration, 118;
  planning permissions of, 118–20
London Brick Land Development
  Co Ltd, 120–21, 129
Longland, Sir Jack, 142, 152
Loveclough Printing Co., 38
Lowe, H. J., 127

Magazine Village, 32
Magnesium Electron Ltd, 40
Mahler, E. A. J., 24, 25
Manchester, dumping by, 64
Manchester Ship Canal, 40
Marine Disposals Ltd, 64–5, 79
Marine Pollution Unit, Burnham-on-
  Crouch, 79
Marine Seaway, 64, 66
Mawddach Estuary, 146–9, 151–3, 159
McKechnie Chemicals Ltd, 54
McLeod, Dr M. C., 17
Medlock, River, 40
Mellanby, Kenneth, 28, 76
Mersey Casings & By-Products Ltd, 53
Mersey Docks and Harbour Board, 58
Mersey and Weaver River Authority, 33, 37, 43, 44, 45, 48;
  conditions of rivers of, 37
Mersey Estuary, 32–6, 53–4, 57–8;
  condition of, 49
Mersey River, 33
Mining, exploration grants for, 132
Misham, E. J., 163
Moore, Dr Norman, 76
Monk's Wood Experimental
  Research Station, 61, 68

Index

Monsanto Chemical Co., 20, 69

Morecambe Bay:
estuarial storage in, 42;
dumping in, 66

Morris, William, 130

National Coal Board, 93–4, 115, 128

National Parks:
origins of, 130–32;
administration of, 142–4;
employment in, 154–7;
threats to, 134–40

National Parks Act, 132, 141

Natural Environment Research Council, 60, 68

Nature Conservancy, 61

Neighbourhood Noise, 107–9

New Brighton, 32, 52

Noble, W. G., 89

Noise:
in coal mines, 93–4;
in cotton mills, 102;
in jute mills, 87, 102;
in foundries, 88–9;
protection from, 98, 99, 100, 109–10, 161;
psychological stresses of, 95–7;
public complaints about, 103

Noise Abatement Act, 1960, 106, 107

Noise Abatement Zones, 107–9

Noise Advisory Council, 107

Noise 'nuisance', 106–7

Noranda-Kerr Ltd, 138

Northumberland National Park, 138

North York Moors National Park, 139

O'Connor, B. A., 58

Oil, sea pollution by, 82–5

Olive's Paper Mill, 39

Pacific Glory, 84

Palmörk, Dr Karsten, 66, 80–81

P.C.B. (poly-chlorinated biphenyls), 61, 63, 67–70

Peak District National Park, 139, 142, 158

Peerless Refining Co., 42

Pembrokeshire Coast National Park, 135

Penalties, 172–3

Perkins Diesel Ltd, 101

Petty, Mrs A., 14, 15

Portman, Dr J. E., 79

Port Tennant Anti-Pollution Association, 3–8

Powell, Watkyn, 151

Price's Chemicals Ltd, 54

Procter & Gamble Ltd, 41

Prosecutions, 12

Purle Bros. Ltd, 64

Qualitex Yarns Ltd, 46

Radcliffe Paper Mill, 38, 47

Ramblers' Association, 143

Ramsbottom Bleaching & Dyeing Co., 39

Ranken, Cmdr Michael, 82–4

Read, C. D., 44

Redcliffe Maud Commission on Local Government, 143

Reservoirs, 44, 135, 138, 140

Resources, 1–2, 165, 169, 170

Rhine, River, 162

Richards, Dickie, 21–2

Rio Tinto-Zinc Corporation, 27–8, 134, 138, 139, 143, 158;
Anglesey smelter, 27–9

Rivers (Prevention of Pollution) Acts, 1951 and 1960, 46, 52–3, 170–71;
pollution powers of, 46

River Pollution Survey of England and Wales, 1970, 34

Roberts, T. M., 15

Robinson, Dr D. W., 98–9

Robinson, T., & Co., 39

Roch, River, 39

Rock Ferry, 32

Rowe, Jeremy, 118, 121, 126
Royal Commission on Environmental Pollution, 35, 162, 171
Royal Society for the Prevention of Cruelty to Animals, 60
Runcorn, sewage of, 49
Ruskin, John, 146

Sainsbury, J. Ltd, 169
Sankey Brook, 41
Scott, Sir Hilary, 107
Scottish Society for the Prevention of Cruelty to Animals, 59
Seabird Wreck in the Irish Sea, Autumn 1969, 59, 68
Secrecy over pollution data, 53, 170–71
Sewage works, 38, 45, 49, 52
Sewerage improvements, 38, 45, 49, 52, 57, 72
Sharp, Gordon, 144–5
Shell Chemicals Ltd, Carrington, 36, 47
Shellfish Association of Great Britain, 36
Shell fisheries, pollution of, 36
Shell (U.K.) Ltd, 56, 139
Silkin, Lewis, 141
Slaughter, Richard, 81
Snowdonia National Park, 138, 144–59; tourism in, 156
Sotheby's, 69
Stella Maris, 72–4
Stewartby Lake scheme, 128–9
Stone Manganese Marine Ltd, 88–9, 99
Stokes v. *G.K.N.*, 88
Sugden, D. B., 89
Sulphur dioxide, pollution, 17, 18, 20
Swincombe reservoir scheme, 135
Switzerland, pollution in, 162, 163

Taken for Granted, 36
Talfourd, Sir T. N., 146
Tattersall, David, 112

Taylor, Rupert, 93, 100, 101
Taylor, Dr William, 87
Taxes on pollution, 169–70
Tees Estuary, 34
Thames Estuary, 34, 35
Thames Board Mills Ltd, 57
Thomas, George, 146–7
Thomas, Martin, 148, 149, 150
Tibenham, Philip, 89
Tinker, Jon, 21, 148
Tolley, J. A., 44
Torrey Canyon, 82, 84
Trade and Industry, Department of, 132–3
Tyne Estuary, 34, 35

Unilever Ltd, 56
United Carbon Black Ltd, 3–8, 26, 104
Union Corporation of South Africa, 138

Veterinary Investigation Service, 15
Vauxhall Motors Ltd, 57

Walker, Peter, Secretary of State for the Environment, 48, 107, 143, 171, 176
Wallasey, sewage of, 52
Ward Blenkinsop Ltd, 54–5
Warrington:
water demand of, 43;
sewage of, 49;
industries of, 57
Water:
demand for, 42–4, 138;
reorganization of services, 48–9
Water Resources Board, 42, 135
Weaver, River, 33, 47
Wells, Ray, 121
Whitby Potash Ltd, 139
Widnes:
sewage of, 49, 57;
industry of, 57
Wokoun, Dr William, 96
Woods, Peter, 68
Wordsworth, William, 130, 146

Yorkshire Dales National Park, 158
Yorkshire Potash Ltd, 139

Zuckerman Commission into Mining and the Environment, 152-3

91
111 4